Abused

Check Everything

**Six more stories
of children murdered by
their parents or caregivers**

Jessica Jackson

This work is based on real cases
*The first part of each story is semi-fictionalised,
with some events and dialogue added*

*The second part tells the facts of each case,
detailing the injuries, trials and sentencing*

Copyright Jessica Jackson © 2023 All rights reserved
No part of this book may be reproduced in any form
without written permission from the author
Reviewers may quote brief passages in reviews

*For the purposes of anonymity, names of
siblings and friends have been changed
unless where commonly known*

This book has details of child abuse
that some readers may find upsetting

Printed by Amazon
In the unlikely event of errors being made during
the printing process, they will be happy to replace your book

Simply go to Your Orders, Replace
and be sure to write 'faulty' across the cover
before returning your book

*Cover Photograph by
Timo Müller at Unsplash
(posed by model)*

Contents

Thank You For Choosing This Book 5
Your Free E-Book 6
This Volume 7
Cinderella and The Prince 9
Singling Out One Child 41
The Family 45
Abusive Families 68
The Perfect Mother 71
Bodily Functions 96
Invitation To My Readers' List 99
Pick Up Your Free E-Book 100
Enter My Draw 101
Thanks To You 102
Playing Dead 103
Prevention of Poppie's Death 139
If You Tell – Buried Alive 143
Choosing a Partner over a Child 165
Surveillance 169
Are They Monsters? 208
Help To Protect Children 212
Your Next Book in the Series 213
Join Us On Facebook 214
Can We Prevent These Murders? 215
Warning Signs of Abuse 216
Don't Miss A Thing 219

Easy Review Codes 220
Acknowledgments 221
Selected Resources 222

Thank You For Choosing This Book

Please proceed with caution if stories of murdered children are likely to deeply upset you.

> If you can spare a moment when you've finished reading, I'd be very grateful if you'd help to raise awareness of child abuse by rating or reviewing this book.

I also have a FREE e-book for you, which you can check out overleaf ...

JESSICA JACKSON

Your Free E-Book

Exclusive only to my readers

**The tragic case
of Isaiah Torres**

*(with bonus content about
Baby Brianna Lopez)*

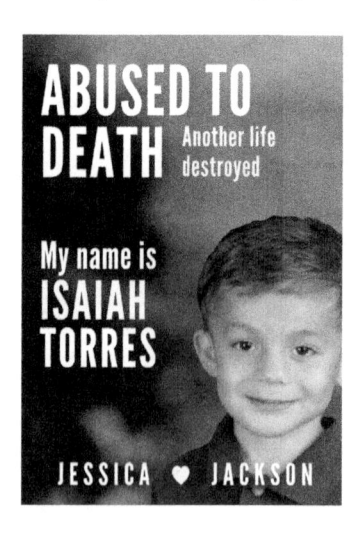

ABUSED TO DEATH Another life destroyed

My name is
ISAIAH TORRES

JESSICA ♥ JACKSON

I'll let you know how to get your copy later

*(Royalties from my books go to
NSPCC, UNICEF and
Prevent Child Abuse America)*

This Volume

Although I am accustomed to immersing myself in the children's suffering in order to tell their stories, writing this volume has opened my eyes wider than ever before, and I have found this collection to be particularly upsetting, as I discover children who were tortured for years.

Sadly, there may never be a shortage of stories to tell, and my ABCD mantra is as relevant as ever:

- A - Assume nothing
- B - Be vigilant
- C - Check everything
- D - Do something

And LISTEN to the children

JESSICA JACKSON

Cinderella and The Prince

'What a day, Elisa!' smiles Miss Ramirez.

I grin back at her. 'I just can't believe it, Miss! What made him choose me?'

'Because you're one of the cleverest children in New York! And when he comes back, you'll have finished writing that story for him, won't you?'

'Oh yes,' I say. '*Will* he come back though, Miss?'

'He said he would. Oh, here's your daddy. Hey, Mr Izquierdo, we're in here!'

I run to him, giggling, and he scoops me up.

'Wooh, somebody's even more excited than usual today.'

'Can I tell him, Miss? Can I tell him?'

'Of course, you can, Elisa.'

'Oh, Daddy, you won't believe it. A man came to school today and he's a prince and I'm going to write him a story and I gave him a big hug and he hugged me back and …'

'Slow down, Mija.' He glances at my teacher. 'A man came and hugged you?'

'It's not what you're thinking, Gustavo,' smiles Miss Ramirez. 'You remember that one of our school patrons is Prince Michael of Greece?'

Daddy nods.

'He paid us a visit today, and this little one followed him everywhere, and she seems to have stolen his heart.'

'Did you behave yourself, Elisa?'

'Oh yes, Daddy. And I didn't really steal his heart!'

'He was really impressed with her, Gustavo. And with how you're raising her on your own.'

It's Daddy's turn to grin. 'Well, I guess I am an amazing father!'

'But seriously, Gustavo. He's offered to pay Elisa's tuition fees!'

'No! Really?'

'Right the way up to 12th grade.'

'I'll be old then,' I say. 'And very very clever.'

'Do you mind if I sit down, Miss Ramirez?'

'I think you'd better!'

'Prince Michael of Greece,' says Daddy. 'Wants to help my daughter's education. It's unbelievable.'

'No, it's really, really true.'

He draws me to him. 'I know, honey. But I never dreamt such a thing was possible.'

'Oh, Daddy! You've always told me that anything's possible if we try hard enough.'

'I guess I did.'

Miss Ramirez brings Daddy a beaker of water. 'You look tired, Gustavo.'

'I'm fine. I'm fine. I guess it's the shock of hearing that my daughter is the Prince's favourite!'

'Is anyone home?'

'Daddy! It's Auntie Carida; can I go answer the door?'

'Sure you can, Princess.'

I stand on my tiptoes to reach the handle.

'Hi, baby girl.'

'Hello, Auntie. Come and see what I did in school today.' I drag her along the hall towards my room. 'I drew something for you.'

'Now isn't that the prettiest picture ever? Who have we got here?'

'It's you, me and Daddy, of course!'

'Oh, yes of course it is! Speaking of your daddy; can I say Hi to my cousin for just one second?' laughs my auntie.

Daddy appears in the doorway. 'Hey, Carida.'

'Hey, cuz. How you doing? Still got that cough?'

'Ah, it's nothing. Stop worrying about me.'

'The lemonade, Daddy. Can we have the lemonade?'

'Of course, Mija. Off you go.'

I run into the kitchen, but I come back quietly when I hear them saying stuff I want to listen to.

'So why aren't they doing anything about it?'

'I don't know, Carida. They seem to think the child's mama can do no wrong.'

'But the bruises, Gus. I've seen a couple more just now.'

'I know. It's breaking my heart. But I don't know what else to do. Even her own family know she's not fit to take care of my baby. Most of them agree with us, Carida.'

My auntie lowers her voice. 'And that Lopez guy. I don't trust him one inch.'

My father puts his finger to his lips. 'Come on back in, Princess. We're getting thirsty in here.'

I hand a beaker of lemonade to Auntie Carida. 'I'll go get ours, Daddy.' I want them to start talking again. I want to hear them say I don't have to go back to visit my mama. I drag my feet, but they've changed the subject.

'Your daddy tells me you've been learning how to dance.'

I twirl round the room. 'Daddy is the best teacher ever.'

'I know, sweetheart. Everyone back home loved the dances he choreographed.'

'Coreo ... what?'

My auntie laughs. 'He made up dances and he danced them with lots of people.'

'Why did you move here, Daddy?'

'Cuba is a poor country, baby. I thought I could have a better life over here.'

My auntie shakes her head. 'So says the janitor!'

Daddy nudges her. 'Watch your mouth, cousin. I do alright. And I'll be teaching dance one day.'

Auntie Carida takes his hand. 'I hope so, Gus. You deserve it.'

Daddy hugs me. 'But I've got my happiness right here.'

I reach up to kiss him, and then kiss Auntie Carida. I love her almost as much as I love Daddy.

'She's ready!' Auntie Carida takes my hand and leads me down to the bottom of the steps, where a cab is waiting.

My dress is gold and blue, and my hair is done up in braids, with ribbons to match my dress.

Daddy gasps when he sees me. 'Oh, my baby!'

'But where are we going, Daddy? I've already had so many lovely surprises today.'

We're still celebrating my baptism, which was last Sunday, and I've had the best day ever. Daddy gave me the Barbie doll I've been gazing at for months in the toy store window. My friends at school made me a special card, and our teacher read us the story of the Mad Hatter's Tea Party from Alice in Wonderland. Juanita kept nudging me and saying, 'If you were having a party, I bet you'd have a better one than that, Elisa.' It made me think that Daddy had planned a big surprise for me.

The surprise is even more fantastic than I imagined. We've come to a place called a banqueting hall, which is a huge room, full of twinkling lights and music. When I can catch my breath, I realise that my best friends and the nice people in my family are all here, smiling at me and clapping. I look up at Daddy and his eyes are shining, almost like he's been crying.

'Come on,' says Auntie Carida. 'Everyone wants to see you.'

I have to be careful walking down the steps in my gold shoes, but my uncles and aunties can't wait for me, and Uncle José grabs me in a hug before I've reached the bottom. I'm passed around the room like a parcel, and I love it! I get so many kisses and 'I love you's' that my throat gets dry with saying thank you and giggling.

'Time for something to eat,' calls Auntie Carida, and everyone moves towards the tables heaped with food. 'Special little girl first.'

I sit between Daddy and my favourite cousin, with crumbs sticking to my chin. The cake is delicious and I'm made to eat two slices all to myself. As if I don't want to!

The music is turned up louder and people are shouting, 'Dance, Elisa! Come on, Elisa, dance!'

Daddy takes my hand, and leads me to the middle of the floor, where he starts to whirl me round in one of the dances he taught me. Soon, all my family and friends are clapping, and they get up to join us on the huge dance floor.

Juanita circles past me. 'I told you you'd have a better party than the Mad Hatter!'

'You were right, Nita!' I yell.

Suddenly, I feel Daddy go limp. 'I'd better sit down now, Mija.'

'I'm tired too, Daddy.' And we go back to our seats, and watch the lights and the colours, as I lie back, safe in my daddy's arms.

'I've got good news, Daddy.'

'Yes, sweetheart?'

'I've decided not to go visit Mama any more! Isn't that a good idea?'

'I'm sorry, baby. But you have to go.'

'But why? Mama isn't nice to me.'

'Oh, my darling. It's just … well, she's your mama.'

'But I don't want to go, Daddy. I really don't.'

'I wish you didn't have to, Mija.'

I cling onto the banister. I know Daddy doesn't want to pull me off, but he gently takes me round the waist.

'Please, for Daddy.'

'I don't like it there!' I say, wrapping my white scarf around my neck. 'And they don't like me, either!'

'But don't you play with your brothers and sisters?'

'Not much. Mama locks me up in the closet!'

'She's doing that again? I thought we'd put a stop to that. I think we'll tell the lady at Children's Welfare again. Should we do that?'

I sigh. If we tell, but I still have to go and stay with Mama and Carlos, they'll hurt me even more. 'I don't know, Daddy. I just don't want to see her anymore. Why do I have to go?'

'It's the law, Princess. Your mama has a right to see you.'

'When I'm older I'll never have to go and see her ever again, will I, Daddy?'

'You won't, honey. And I'm going to phone right now to tell about them. Don't worry, darling. I'm going to make everything right.'

'Will we be in trouble for being late?'

'Shh, honey. It's ringing at the other end.' He clears his throat. 'Yes, it's Gustavo Izquierdo for Miss Ribera. Yes, I'll hang on.'

He blows me a kiss. 'Yes, I know; she's due to be there at four o'clock, but she's telling me again that they're locking her in a closet.' He puts the phone closer to his mouth and almost whispers. 'And she's soiling the bed as well as wetting it now. She never did anything like that before.' He turns to check if I'm listening. 'She's scared of going. I don't want her to go. At least don't make her stay overnight. Please! They're hurting my daughter. What? No, you can't do that! I've done nothing wrong.' He coughs harshly. 'Excuse me, yes, go on. Alright, alright, if we have no choice. But I want something to be done about it soon!'

He puts the phone on the counter. 'Come on, baby. We have to go.'

'Daddy, are you crying?'

'Of course not, silly! Come on, let's get this over with, and you'll be back home before we know it!'

In my dream, they're both chasing me, and I'm running, but I can't escape from the house. Every door I get to is locked, though I can hear my brothers and sisters playing inside the rooms. I reach the front door but my hands are dripping with sweat and blood and I can't turn the handle.

My mother is laughing. 'Stupid girl,' she says.

And then *he* grabs me. His hands are clammy as he rubs them all over my body.

'Daddy, help me,' I cry.

They're both laughing now. 'Daddy can't help you! We can do whatever we want with you!'

'No!' I scream, and suddenly the hands are soft and gentle, and Aunt Carida is saying, 'It's just a bad dream, sweetheart. Auntie's here.'

I'm shivering and sobbing.

'Hush, baby girl. It's alright now. I'm here. I'm here.'

I feel the dampness from my waist to my ankles. 'Did I do it again?'

My aunt Carida nods. 'But it's okay. Don't worry, darling.'

'I'm sorry, Auntie.'

She holds me tight. 'Everything's going to be alright. I promise. Come on, we'd better get you cleaned up. Have you forgotten that your daddy and me are taking you to the circus today?'

'I've got them, Gus!' Aunt Carida waves the tickets in the air.

'The 26th?'

'Yes, the 26th. You'll be out of here and our little Princess won't have to go *there* anymore. Oh, I wish I was coming with you.'

'Please come, Auntie,' I say. 'I will hardly know anyone there.'

'What? All your cousins can't wait to see you, and show you their games.'

'Your auntie is right, Elisa. We're going to have a fantastic time.' Daddy coughs and reaches for his handkerchief. 'But don't forget, it's a secret for now.'

'I won't tell anyone. And is it really as beautiful as you've told me?'

'Of course! One of the first places we'll go to is Zapata, to see the crocodiles!'

'Gus!' says Aunt Carida. 'You'll scare the child! Don't worry, Cuba has many places without crocodiles!'

'Like the beaches,' I say. 'Daddy says I'll learn to swim, didn't you, Daddy?'

'You'll have to teach *me* first!' Daddy laughs and starts to cough again.

'What can I do for you, Gus?' My auntie touches his arm gently.

'Nothing,' splutters Daddy. 'I'm fine.'

'Shall I go and start packing my clothes and toys, Daddy?'

'Not yet, Mija. There's still a little while before we need to do that.'

'Come with me, sweetheart,' says my auntie. 'I'll take you to the bathroom.'

'No, Auntie!'

'I'm sorry, honey. I need to check you aren't hurting down there again.'

'Please don't. Daddy, please don't let anyone touch me.'

'Okay, Princess. It's okay. Does it hurt there though?'

I don't like lying to Daddy, but I've been told not to tell. 'Of course not, Daddy!'

'Elisa, we want to help you,' says Aunt Carida.

I scream when she tries to take my arm.

'Carida!' says Daddy. 'It's okay. We'll be leaving soon. We can hang on just a little longer.'

'I'm sorry to have upset you, baby,' says my auntie.

'It's okay, Auntie.' I climb up onto her knee. 'Hug me, please.'

She looks across at Daddy. 'You're doing the right thing, Gustavo.'

'But when is he coming back?'

Aunt Carida squeezes me closer. Her cheeks are wet and burning hot.

'You'll see him again some day, Mija.'

'No, I want to see him now! I want my daddy!'

'Put her to bed, Carida,' says one of her cousins.

'No, I want her beside me. She needs to feel safe.'

Everyone's black clothes make them look sad, and most of them are crying. If Daddy was here, he'd start dancing and make them smile again.

'Aren't we going to Cuba now, Auntie?'

'Oh, baby. No, I don't think so.'

'We can still go. Daddy will ask them to change the date on the tickets.'

That makes her cry again.

'And when Daddy comes back, he'll still want to take me. We were so excited to go there.'

'I know, Mija. I know.'

'I don't mind waiting until he gets better.' I know his cough was making him real sick, and that we might have to wait until he gets good medicine to make it better.

'Tell her, Carida.'

Auntie takes me onto her knee. 'My precious girl.' She lifts up my chin to look into my eyes. 'Daddy isn't going to come back. His cough couldn't get better, so God has taken him to heaven.'

'Oh, that's okay. If God is taking care of him, he'll soon be okay, and he'll come back home.'

Auntie Carida buries her face into my hair. She makes a little moaning noise, and my hair is getting wet.

'Don't worry, Auntie. Daddy will come back and take me to Cuba.'

But soon I have to accept that Daddy isn't coming back from heaven just yet, and we're not going to Cuba, and I cry for days and days.

'Why does Mama hurt us?'

The judge wouldn't let Auntie Carida take care of me, and I'm living with my mama and her husband. I don't like it here.

I've been allowed to share my half-sister's bedroom tonight, but we're not supposed to talk to each other.

'I don't know,' she whispers. 'It's always been like this.'

'What does she do to you?'

'Just beating.' She reaches out for my hand. 'Not the things she does to you.'

'Why does she want us to live with her when she doesn't like us?'

'I think it's the drugs. They send her crazy.'

'I miss my daddy. And my aunties. I hope they'll come and get me.'

'Elisa.'

'Yes?'

'They're not coming for you, sweetheart. Your daddy's dead.'

I bow my head. 'I know that's what they say, but he'd never leave me. Never.'

My sister hugs me.

'He was going to take me to Cuba.'

'You'd have been safe there, Elisa.'

The welts on my arms hurt where she holds me. I don't care.

'And she won't let your auntie come and see you. I've seen her outside the apartment a few times now, but Carlos chases her off.'

'If I was allowed to look out of the window, I could see her. I'd love to see her. Just once.'

'I know. You look tired, Elisa.'

'I'm so hungry and thirsty. But Mama beats me when I say I want a drink.'

'What's that noise in there?'

We freeze.

'Get out here, you filthy, little whore.'

I'm scared to. But I know I have to.

'In the cupboard. Now! We'll see to you later.'

My sister stretches out her hand, but we both know there's nothing she can do.

The neighbour is banging on the door.

'What the hell are you doing to those kids? I'll call Child Welfare again.'

My mother laughs. 'You think they'll believe you this time? I could whack her right in front of them and they'd say I was doing my best to be the perfect Mama!'

'I'm still calling them.'

'You do that, and I'll throw her out the window.'

The neighbour pauses. Mama continues to stab her cigarette on my arm.

'Awilda,' says the neighbour. 'If you don't want the kids, let someone else take them.'

'Not much fun in that,' says my mother, and bashes my head against the wall.

'I'm calling them!' And I hear the footsteps going down the hall.

Mama cackles with laughter. 'You hear that, Carlos? The idiot thinks Child Welfare are going to come and look at the kids.'

Her husband's face comes into view. 'Shall we give them something to investigate? Where's the hairbrush, honey?'

They use it on my private parts. Daddy told me no one should touch them, apart from gently washing them. My screams seem to shake the apartment. I can't bear it. I just can't.

'She's shit herself again, Awilda.'

'I think she likes to eat it, don't you? Or why would she do it?'

'Eat, mongoloid. Eat it.'

My mother is laughing so hard she starts to choke.

My face is in my own mess. I can hardly breathe. *Daddy, I wish I was with you.*

'Not so pretty now, are you, whore? Not so damn clever!'

One of them bangs my head into the concrete wall. I slump against it in a daze. I just want to be with Daddy.

My mother and stepfather are shouting again. This time, it's not at me, or any of the other children.

My mother screams. 'Get away, you animal. I'm bleeding. I'm bleeding. I'm calling the cops.'

The cops take my stepfather away for stabbing my mother. Perhaps it'll be a little quieter now.

It's November when my mother throws me into the concrete wall again. As usual, she throws me head first. I think she does it more than once. I'm screaming. Louder and louder. My throat gets hoarse and when I swallow it tastes like blood.

I'm lying on the bed. I can't see and sounds are strange. There is liquid dripping from my ears and nose.

I hear my mother come into the room. She's on the phone to her sister. 'She's just retarded on the bed. No, she won't eat or drink anything.' She comes closer. 'No, not yet. I'll think about it. I'm in the middle of cleaning the dishes right now. No, she'll be fine. She's been like this before.'

The pain in my head is agony. 'Mama,' I try to whisper.

But my mother leaves the room.

My eyes are closed but I can feel a warm light washing over me. Gentle and welcoming. 'Daddy, are you there?'

The fluid from my ears is now just a trickle, and I can hear Daddy's voice. 'I'm here, my Princess. I'm here.'

'Don't leave me, Daddy.'

'I won't Mija.'

'I've been so frightened.'

'There's no need to be frightened anymore. I'm here, Mija.'

'They said you'd gone away for ever.'

'I've come back. I've come to take you with me.'

'But I'm so dirty. And I smell. They won't let me wash.'

I hear Daddy chuckle. 'Don't worry, sweetheart.'

'I don't think I can walk, Daddy.'

'It will all be made better when you come with me, Princess.'

'Will you brush my hair like you used to?'

'Until it shines, Elisa.'

'Oh, Daddy, I've missed you so much.'

'And I have missed you too.'

'Will we see Auntie Carida?'

'Not today. Not yet. But a little later, Mija.'

'Daddy, will you hold me?'

'Come to me, my angel. I'm going to take care of you now.'

An Overview of Elisa's Case

Elisa Izquierdo
11.02.89 – 22.11.95
aged 6 years & 9 months
New York, USA

Elisa was born in Brooklyn, New York, to Gustavo Izquierdo and Awilda Lopez.

Elisa's father had immigrated from Cuba in search of a better life, and was working as a cleaner and cook at a homeless shelter, until he could get his business as a dance teacher off the ground. Evicted for being unable to pay her rent, Awilda Lopez became a resident at the shelter, and she and Gustavo formed a relationship.

Due to her crack-cocaine addiction, Lopez' two older children had been taken into the custody of her family, and when Gustavo discovered that his girlfriend had begun using again during the pregnancy with his daughter, he ended the relationship. Baby Elisa was born addicted to the drug, and her father gained full custody.

It is poignant to note that on the day Gustavo brought his baby home from the hospital, he rang several friends in a panic, asking how to change her diaper and prepare formula. Having no experience of parenthood, he wanted to learn all he could about how to care for his daughter. He also attended parenting classes at the local YWCA.

Gustavo took Elisa everywhere; to the circus, to the movies, and to the park. He carried many photographs of her in his wallet, and relatives, friends and neighbours remarked how proud he was to walk down the street with his little girl, that he painstakingly brushed her hair and tied it into plaits, and that he called her his princess.

Raised in this way by her loving father, and with her father's cousin, Elsa (Aunt Carida) Canizares, and other family members showering the little girl with love and affection, her early years were full of joy and safety. On celebration days, Gustavo threw wonderful parties for her, including the hiring of a banqueting hall for her baptism at the age of four.

Wanting the best for his child, Gustavo enrolled Elisa at the Montessori pre-school. She was thriving and happy, but her father's health was deteriorating, and he found himself unable to pay the school fees. But his devotion, along with Elisa's outstanding ability, had caught the attention of one of the school's patrons, Prince Michael of Greece, who offered to pay for her private education at the Brooklyn Friends School, right up until 12th grade. The charming friendship continued throughout Elisa's short life, with the two exchanging gifts and notes.

In the meantime, Awilda Lopez entered rehab, got married, obtained permanent accommodation, and regained full custody of her two older children. From November 1991, she was permitted to have unsupervised visits from Elisa on alternate weekends.

And Elisa's abuse began.

Pleas from both Gustavo and Elisa's teachers, stating that she returned from these visits bruised and upset, vomiting and refusing to go into the bathroom, fell on deaf ears at the Child Welfare Agency. Her genitalia were damaged, and, suffering terrible nightmares, she began to be doubly incontinent. Her siblings also told relatives that their half-sister was being locked away and beaten.

Even severely brutalised children rarely express that they don't want to see their abusing parent anymore, but a desperate Elisa announced this very explicitly–and was overruled by the agencies who could have saved her.

The next part of Elisa's story makes me tearful every time I think of it. But here I go.

Gustavo made plans to return to his native Cuba with his daughter. I don't have categorical evidence whether this was to remove Elisa from her mother's clutches or not. He booked tickets in readiness for departure on 26 May 1994. But earlier in the month, his declining health led to a hospital visit, and, at the age of 39, he died of lung cancer on the very day they were due to travel. Had he lived just a few more days, and been able to make the journey, Elisa could have perhaps been raised by relatives in Cuba and never known the horrors of unbelievable torture. Had the devoted young father not been stricken by cancer at all, I can only imagine the joyful life they would both have led.

After Gustavo's death, those who cared about Elisa and feared for her safety sprang into action to prevent Lopez being granted full custody of her daughter. Awilda Lopez was initially awarded temporary custody, during which time her aunt, her schoolteachers, and Prince Michael of Greece attempted to intercede for Elisa, writing letters to the judge, Phoebe Greenbaum, about her mother's cruelty.

Elisa's aunt applied for custody in her own right, but without legal representation and in the face of Lopez' legal aid funded lawyer, she was forced to listen to testimony that praised the torturer's "valiant attempts" to avoid returning to drug abuse, false claims that Elisa wanted to live with her mother, and reprimands at her own temerity at having "the nerve" to remove the little girl from her biological mother. The distraught woman replied that "the nerve" was borne of the fear of what would happen to Elisa.

Prince Michael later looked back on his own attempts to save Elisa, saying: "There was a solution. There were people ready to take this child–to love this child."

This is not the first time I have written about the unbearable pain of loving relatives being pushed out of the picture, knowing in their hearts that the child they long to care for is going to be neglected and abused. Or worse.

Lopez was awarded full and permanent custody of Elisa in September 1994, condemning the child to a year of horror, pain and misery.

Her first act was to withdraw her daughter from the private school that Prince Michael was happy to continue paying for, where she was thriving, popular and happy, and send her to a local public school. This act alone gives us a glimpse into Awilda Lopez' attitude towards her daughter. My assumption is that she was jealous of the chance Elisa had been given, a chance which she herself had not had when she was a child. A nurturing parent would have been proud and happy at this opportunity. But Lopez instead removed Elisa from the school immediately, perhaps with the intention to 'put her in her place'. Looking at photographs of beautiful, vibrant Elisa, I can't help but feel that Lopez was insanely jealous of her in every way.

Staff at her new school soon noticed that the five-year-old was often uncommunicative, incontinent, and pulled out clumps of her hair. How different to the sweet, confident and intelligent child she had been when in her father's care. The school reported their concerns to the Manhattan Child Welfare Authorities, who found these to be 'unreportable' due to a lack of clear evidence. Elisa was also supposedly under the care of a court-appointed caseworker.

To further sabotage Elisa's well-being, ***Lopez withdrew her from school altogether*** (where have we heard that before!) in December 1994. Elisa was no longer under the eye of caring teaching staff, and as usual, no checks were made as to her safety. Little did they know that the bright and intelligent child was being locked in a dark room or cupboard for hours or days at a time.

Lopez, who by now had six children, was said to be abusing drugs again. I have found conflicting reports as to the abuse of the other children, but my understanding is that they *were* abused, though not as severely as Elisa. Needless to say, being witnesses to their sister's torture must have been excruciating.

In addition to being locked up for long periods, and isolated from her siblings, Elisa endured many painful tortures and indignities by her mother and her stepfather, Carlos Lopez.

She was turned upside down, with her hair and face then used as a mop to clean the floor. Later, they cut off her beautiful hair. She was denied access to the bathroom and made to consume her own bodily waste. The six-year-old was sexually abused, vaginally and anally, with a hairbrush and a toothbrush. When they fractured her shoulder, she suffered for three days before being taken to hospital.

There are claims, that I can neither prove nor disprove, that the mother slid snakes down her daughter's throat.

Awilda Lopez called her child a 'mongoloid' and a 'filthy little whore'.

Elisa was bright and articulate, and could have helped around the home and with her three younger siblings. She was bubbly and loving; so what made her mother want to crush that out of her so brutally and completely, when instead she could have had her own problems made lighter with a smile and a hug from her daughter? Awilda Lopez seemed intent on destroying her daughter. And that's exactly what she did.

On that fateful November day, Lopez threw her daughter head first into a concrete wall. From that moment, Elisa lay dying. The following day, as brain fluid leaked from Elisa's nose and ears, Awilda Lopez brought a neighbour into the home to show her Elisa's body. When Lopez refused to call the police, the neighbour did so herself, with Lopez going up onto the roof of the apartment building and threatening to jump to her death. The mother of six was talked down, and the following day, she was arrested.

As well as the head injury that killed Elisa, the autopsy reported broken fingers, toes, damage to internal organs, deep welts, burns across her head, face and body. Her genitalia were swollen, torn and scarred due to the anal and vaginal violations she endured.

Elisa's funeral was attended by more than 300 people, including the then mayor of New York City, Rudolph Giuliani, and Elisa's royal friend, Prince Michael of Greece. Both the maternal and paternal sides of Elisa's family wanted to bury Elisa where they chose, and the funeral home sided with her murderer's family. I do not doubt that there were members of this side of the family who loved and cherished Elisa too. I wonder what Elisa would have chosen if we could have asked her. Nevertheless, the words on her gravestone are poignant and very apt: "***World, please watch over the children.***"

I cannot find much information about Awilda's upbringing. Whether her unbridled cruelty sprang from an abusive childhood, an innate predisposition to inflict horrors upon the vulnerable, a mind altered by her drug abuse, or a combination of them all, we will perhaps never know.

Prior to her trial and sentencing, Awilda Lopez was interviewed in jail, by talk show host, Rolonda Watts. As

I've mentioned before, we can learn so much from the murderers themselves, with a view to preventing further deaths, but little was gleaned here. Lopez claimed that she had never subjected Elisa to any form of abuse apart the occasional spanking. (There's that word again. If it wasn't so unbearably tragic, it would be laughable. That magic word that every abusive parent trots out, because they think that 'spanking' in whatever way they choose to interpret and administer it, is okay.)

During that interview, I did not see Lopez express sorrow that her child was dead. At 29 years old, the thin woman with gappy tombstone teeth repeated several times that she didn't kill her daughter. No sadness that her daughter was dead, nor an explanation of how she could have died. Just denial.

"I used to hit her. I used to spank her *and everything*. But I didn't kill her." Those are my italics. *And everything*. We know some of the horrors that lie behind those two words.

One of the neighbours who, through the walls, heard the sounds of abuse along with Elisa begging for mercy, makes a statement that is a sad reflection upon how we collude in violence to children: "We thought it was simply her way of disciplining her kids. That's not unusual, in this building at least".

Well, that is something we all need to change.

When there are witnesses to the torture, as in the case here of Elisa's half siblings, we are given a truer picture of the lengths the murderers go to. Without their presence, we would never have known that a precious human being was so humiliated that she was used as a broom to brush the floor. How many other untold cruelties are dreamt up by the perpetrators of child murder by abuse?

Just a few weeks after the interview with Rolonda, Lopez was pleading guilty to second degree murder, and allegedly showing remorse. In June 1996, Awilda Lopez was sentenced to fifteen years to life. Judge Schlesinger had these words to say: "We have not created procedures to do everything necessary to protect the young and vulnerable in this society. The system has failed to protect our babies, and don't tell me how much it costs. If anything is to become of this horrendous tragedy, [then] it will be that we give priority to these babies."

With all requests for parole denied up to this point (January 2023) Awilda Lopez remains in the maximum security Bedford Hills Correctional Facility for Women.

Awilda's husband, Carlos Lopez, who wasn't present at the time of Elisa's death, due to being in prison, was sentenced to 1-3 years for the abuse of the little girl, namely one instance of banging her head repeatedly against a concrete wall.

I attempt to keep personal criticism out of my stories. Readers of Volume 2 may recall that I allowed myself to show my feelings towards a judge who freed two murderers after 3-4 years because *their crime was so heinous they weren't likely to commit such an outrage again.*

Phoebe Greenbaum is another judge with incomprehensible views. Despite the mother's drug abuse, the injuries reported by numerous people, and the wishes of her dying father, the judge awarded custody of Elisa to her abuser. Greenbaum responded to this criticism by claiming that she had been merely following procedural recommendations when she had made her custodial decision. I suppose she has to justify her decision somehow.

In the aftermath of Elisa's murder, due to the confidentiality procedures at the time, welfare staff were not obliged to answer probing questions regarding their collective role. Frustration at this refusal brought about two major changes:

Rudolph Giuliani quickly began a review of the city's child welfare system, which in due course, inspired the creation of the Administration for Children's Services—focused purely on child welfare in New York.

And on February 12, 1996, Governor George Pataki formally signed Elisa's Law into legislation.

This law ensures that when a child who was known to the authorities is then abused to death, reports on the agencies' actions are made available for public scrutiny. Although the reports do not name the deceased child, nor the particular social workers involved, they list every complaint made and the agency's response, along with an assessment as to whether the overall response was good enough. Too late for the child, of course.

Rest Safely in Peace, Elisa

To avoid confusion with the two very similar names, in my story, I have used the name 'Carida' (Spanish for kindness), for Elisa's loving aunt. She was in fact called 'Elsa', and I wonder if Elisa was named in her honour. I mean no disrespect to Elsa's family for the name change.

Singling Out One Child

Elisa's case highlights the fact that a child's murder springs from a combination of the most utterly tragic set of circumstances.

Awilda Lopez had six children. She had a choice of children to single out for torture, and I feel there are several reasons she focused on Elisa.

It appears that Lopez had already been abusing the children she had in her custody. But as the newest arrival, the abuse quickly became centred on Elisa. Awilda Lopez may have resented Elisa's father for ending the relationship during her pregnancy, and used that, consciously or not, as a reason to torture Gustavo's child.

I cannot ignore the possibility of jealousy playing a huge part. Lopez had certainly lost any good looks she may have had as a child and teenager, and she may have become insanely jealous of this version of her younger self. Coupled with that, are the opportunities her daughter had been given when she herself had had none.

Having experienced their own chaotic and violent childhood, some perpetrators have a deep and overwhelming self hatred that they transfer onto the child version of themselves, punishing them in ways equal to and beyond what had been done to them. This is most common when the child is the same gender as the abuser, as in this case. And does the power the abuser has now, compel them to punish and torture, when as a child they were utterly powerless?

Whatever the case, this gifted and bright little girl was loved unconditionally by her doting father, who tried to protect her from her mother's extraordinary cruelty. Had her father lived, Elisa would have blossomed into the confident and beautiful girl she was destined to be.

Montessori Schooling

From the age of one, Elisa attended the Montessori pre-school, where she would have had her needs met in a nurturing way that allowed her to develop and grow, both educationally and emotionally. Here's a little background with the Montessori method, if you are unfamiliar with it.

In the early 20th century, Maria Montessori, an Italian physician, developed a method of encouraging children to learn at their own pace, in a hands-on manner, promoting their independence and focusing on their natural interests rather than impressing formal teaching upon them.

Maria Montessori believed that education has a vital part to play in working towards world peace, and published 'Education and Peace' in 1936. She also gained the interest of Mahatma Ghandi. But her methods were not widely accepted by the traditional teaching systems at the time, and opportunities were lost. There was, however, a resurgence of her methods after her death, and the 'Montessori Method' is now used all over the world, in both public and private schools, primarily with children aged up to six years old, when their minds are developing the most quickly.

Footnote: Elsa Canizares (Aunt Carida in the story), who longed to care for little Elisa, passed away in 2007, at the age of 44.

Rest in peace Elsa, with Gustavo and Elisa

JESSICA JACKSON

The Family

(For information, Ame is pronounced the same as the usual spelling of Amy)

Story-time is my favourite part of the day. We all sit on the floor and cross our legs. The teacher sits on a low stool and opens the book. I can see the colour of the pictures inside as she turns the first page. Everyone goes quiet, and I hold my breath.

'Ame. Ame, sweetheart.' Someone is shaking my shoulder.

I wake up to my teacher's smiling face.

'Sorry, Miss.'

'That's okay. But what's making you so tired these days?'

I still feel drowsy. 'Cartoons, Miss.'

'Cartoons?'

'Yes, we stayed up late to watch them last night.' I'm getting good at this. 'They were so funny!'

She smiles. 'My kids like cartoons, Ame. Which ones were they?'

Everyone is looking at me. 'Uhm, uhm. I can't remember.'

'But you enjoyed them, that's the main thing. Try and get a good night's sleep tonight though, won't you?'

'I will, Miss. I'm sorry, Miss.'

'Right, everyone, it's home-time. Remember to collect your pencils and lunchboxes.'

I hang around the cubbies, trying to look busy.

One of the boys pulls my hair. 'I don't know why you're pretending you've even got a lunchbox, Deal. Everybody knows you haven't!'

'I just forgot it again today,' I whisper.

'Stop telling lies, Deal.'

'I'm sorry.'

My brother taps my shoulder. 'You okay, Ame?'

'Yes, I'm fine,' I say.

'He shouldn't say things like that, sis.'

'Don't worry about it.'

'Okay, I'm off to play football. See you later, Ame.'

My little cousin puts her hand in mine; just for a moment. 'Hey, Ame.'

'Hey, sweetheart.'

She snatches her hand away, just in case our aunt is hiding behind the school gates.

My aunt *is* there, and she shoves me to the back as usual, and I walk behind everyone. She asks the other kids about their day in school, but I don't think she listens as they bob up and down, telling her about the pictures they drew and the stories they heard.

Back home, we all queue up to go past another of my aunties.

'Anything to tell me?' she snaps at each of us in turn.

We shake our heads and mutter. 'No, Auntie. It's all good.'

'You know what I mean,' she says, not allowing my little cousin to pass. 'Her. Has she been talking?'

'I don't think so, Auntie.'

'You don't think so? You know what I think? I think that means she's been talking and needs to be punished.'

'No, Auntie. She didn't …' My cousin looks at me, and mouths, 'Sorry,' as I start to tremble.

My uncle comes into the room.

'Deal with her,' says Auntie.

My uncle grabs my arm and drags me into their room. 'What have you been told about being naughty and disobedient?'

'I'm sorry.'

'Too late for sorry, Ame. You should behave yourself in the first place.'

'I know, I'm sorry.'

He reaches for the 'butt buster'.

'Please, Uncle. I already hurt so much.'

'That's because you're so fucking bad, Ame. You need discipline every day now.'

'I'm sorry.'

He whacks me with the heavy wooden paddle until I'm screaming.

'Right, where's the box?'

'Please, please don't put me in there. Please, Uncle.'

'You know you're going in there, so why do you keep whining? You know I can't stand whining.'

'I didn't mean to, I'm sorry, I'm sorry.'

'Cyn,' he yells. 'Cyn, bring the box.'

The box is a plastic storage container my sister used to keep her Barbie things in. It's less than three feet long and about a foot wide and deep. It's the worst punishment. Worse than the backbends or eating pooh.

'What's she been up to this time?' says Auntie Cynthia as she brings the box in.

'Does it matter? She's just a bad girl.'

'Get in,' she says.

I try my best, I really do. But I'm too big, though I'm only four feet two. But I know I somehow have to fit myself in, so I climb in and lie on my side with my legs curled up to my chest. My uncle pushes me further down so that he can get the lid on.

'Padlock, Cyn.'

'Right here.'

'It's so hot,' I say quietly. 'Let me out and I'll be good. I'll do anything you say.'

'You hear something?' says my auntie.

My uncle grunts.

'Me neither. Let's go get some lemonade.'

I imagine a nice cool drink of lemonade sliding down my throat. And a popsicle. That's even better, because you can hold it in your mouth, feeling its ice seeping into the dry places, until it slowly melts away.

The plastic of the box is pressing into my skin, into the same places it pressed into last time, where the sores have come up. *Please, please, God. Don't let me be in here for long this time.*

I can tell Auntie Cyn's footsteps as she comes back into the room.

'Please, Auntie.'

She kicks the box. 'Shut up, idiot.'

Suddenly, the lid presses down even harder, and I feel I'm going to be squashed flat. I hear her tapping on her laptop keys. She's sitting on the box and playing on her computer. She can play these games for hours.

'Auntie!' I scream as loud as I can. 'Auntie, let me out. I can't breathe.'

She raises herself up and for a second I dare to hope it's all over. But she bounces back down again, heavier than ever.

'If you couldn't breathe, you couldn't yell like that, so just shut the fuck up.'

My eyes are burning. I can't even cry. I'm so thirsty and dry; I don't think I have any tears left. I try to think about nice things, like school and how the teachers all like me and are kind to me. I'm learning lots of things and I try to remember some of them, because I want to get a good job when I'm grown up. I'll go far away from here. But I'm only nine years old, and that's a long time to wait.

'Mommy,' I whisper in my mind. 'Mommy, will you come for me?'

My uncle comes back and I hear them talking about letting me out.

'You think she's learned her lesson?'

I don't know what lesson they mean, but they know I did something bad.

'Not quite. Roll her around a little. Just to make sure.'

After a few rolls, I start to feel sick, but I'm terrified that if I do they'll make me eat it again.

It's dark when they finally unclasp the lock.

'Bed!' they say, and I curl myself up in the shower stall.

The next day, my teacher spots the marks on my arms. 'What's this, Ame?'

'Oh, I don't know.' She's taken me by surprise and I've forgotten what they told me to say. Why on earth did I pull up my sleeves? 'I guess I got them when I was play-fighting with my brother.'

'You sure about that, Ame?'

'Oh yes, Miss. I remember now.' I laugh. 'We got into such a fight. Grandma had to separate us.'

'These look like finger marks, honey.'

'I know, that's what he does. Squeezes real tight. He got in trouble for that.' I'm in my stride now; I can see in my head what could've happened. 'My dad shouted at him. But he didn't spank him. We don't do that in our family.'

'You quite sure about that, Ame?'

'Oh yes, Miss. Quite sure.' I wriggle my arm out of her grasp. 'Can I go play now, Miss?'

Of course, there's no one to play with me at recess. My brothers and sisters won't go that far in disobeying the grownups, and the other kids say I smell, so I hang around by the bins as usual. When no one's looking, I'm able to grab a half-eaten sandwich. It's delicious; even though the mayo seems to have gone off a bit. Some days there's candy in the bins, and once I found a full Twinkie.

My brother scoots up as I'm gulping down the last bite. 'Did you tell her anything?'

'No, of course not.'

'You know what'll happen if anyone finds out?'

'Yeah, I do. It's okay, I told her we were fighting.'

'Good. That's good. If you say anything, they'll take us all away to other families. And we'll get beat real hard every day. Even the babies.'

I shake my head. 'I'll never tell, I promise.' But I wonder if going to another family would be better for me than how things are at home.

I've been allowed to sit in the shade for a while, watching the other kids play. The little ones are so funny, running around in just their diapers, squealing with laughter.

When a vehicle pulls out front, I don't think it can be a visitor for us. Our folks have rusty old station wagons, not shiny new cars.

'Get indoors, Ame,' says Grandma, and I'm off in a flash.

Most of the grown-ups gather on the porch.

'We've had some more complaints, ma'am,' says a tall woman in glasses.

'Oh, really? What about?'

'Neglecting these kids. Beating on them. Some other stuff.'

'Well now, unless you're an officer of the law, I don't believe you can do nothing about that!'

Auntie Cyn notices me at the window and flaps her hand to shoo me away.

After a few minutes and some raised voices, the smart car drives off, and everyone springs into action, throwing stuff into cases and boxes.

'Ame, put the dogs in their cages.'

'What's going on?'

'Just do it!'

And by the next morning we've moved to Phoenix, Arizona.

If Mommy comes looking for me, I wonder how she'll find me now.

This time, we don't go to school. Grandma's set up a couple of tables in the garage and some of the kids sit around reading books and writing. When I get to join in, they just make me write the same things over and over: 'I will answer when talked to,' and 'I will not steal food from the little ones'.

Sometimes Bella pads into the schoolroom when I'm writing and I pet her head, and if no one's watching, I scoot down from my seat and give her a big hug. I sometimes think she's trying to tell me that she loves me. We've had her from a pup, and she's my best friend.

Arizona is really hot. It's harder for me here, because no one lets me drink to quench my thirst and they even watch me if I try to sneak water from the toilet. I feel dizzy all the time, and sometimes I even feel shivery, even though I'm dripping with sweat. It's hard to do my chores, because I feel so weak and fall over.

My big cousin kicks me. 'Get up, lazy.'

I press my hands into the ground and try to push myself up. My hands slide along the floor and I fall onto my face.

She laughs. 'Up!'

I try again, this time falling hard onto my chin.

My cousin puts her lips close to my ear. 'If you don't get up right now, you're going to be outside all night.'

I'm shivering and almost passing out, but I have to get up. I grab the side of a chair and pull myself up to a standing position. I feel like my legs won't hold me.

'Outside!'

'But I managed it!'

'Not quick enough. Now get out.'

The sun is beating down on the sidewalk as she forces me to walk up and down in my bare feet. My skin is burning and I can feel the blisters forming and bursting.

My cousin and her husband sit on the wall, sipping juice. 'Keep going, girl.'

A neighbour comes out of her house, setting off to walk her dog. She glances at me, then puts her head down as she passes me.

I'm hobbling along the sidewalk. The heat from the sun is scorching every part of me, my ears are buzzing, and I feel as if I'm constantly on the edge of fainting. I pray for it to be over, but my cousin keeps telling me to carry on. The sweat from the hair that's plastered to my forehead is pouring into my eyes, and I can't see where I'm going. I hold onto the fence to guide and support me. A sip of water would be heavenly. My head swims and I fall against the fence.

'For fuck's sake,' yells my cousin. But she lets me stop.

'Thank you, Auntie. Oh, thank you!' It's another hot day, and we've all been given popsicles for doing our chores. Mmm, it feels lovely just to hold it in my hand.

'What you doing with that, Ame?' It's my big cousin again.

'We all got them. We did our chores real well.'

'I don't think so!' she hollers and grabs it out of my hand. 'You stole it, you nasty little liar!'

'I didn't, I promise. I didn't.'

'Get into position.'

I lie on my back, then raise my body up off the floor, arching my back, my hands and feet supporting me. The kids call it 'the crab'. I hope it won't be for long because I know this hurts after a couple of minutes.

'Can I stop now, please?'

'You can not. You're a thief and a liar and you're going to be punished real good.'

'It hurts. It really hurts.' My whole body is burning. My arms feel like they're coming out of their sockets.

'Stay up there, girl.'

After a few minutes, I can't hold my weight up anymore and I droop down towards the floor.

Her husband slaps me and then puts me back up into position.

'I can't do it. I'm trying but I just can't.' I'm crying with the pain, and sweat is dripping onto the floor.

'You can do it, and you will do it. You will do as you're told, once and for all.'

I always do as I'm told, always. I'm too scared not to. But it doesn't do any good.

'Right, time for the box.'

'No!' My throat is dry and my voice is hoarse, but I can't go in there tonight. I can't bear the heat. I heard on the news the temperature is over 100.

'Get her in. I don't want to see that stupid face.'

The box is still smelly and wet from the last time, and they really have to cram me in. I'm almost face-down and the grooves of the box immediately press against me. If they don't let me out after five minutes, it's going to be the worst one ever. I just know it.

'Please, oh please, let me out.'

But they don't listen. They clip the padlock on and flip the box over a few times, laughing. 'Thief! You stole a popsicle, you little thief!'

The sweat is running into my eyes. I can't breathe. I'm scared. So scared. I try to bang on the box but I can't move my arms. I push my feet against the sides but there's just no room. I wish I could fall asleep until it's over. I feel the box being lifted up and I try to shout. I'm being carried into the garage. *No, please no.* The garage is the hottest place ever.

I can hear my little cousins running about outside the garage, squealing when someone gets caught in the game of tag they're playing. Bella is snuffling around the box and I try to speak to her, but my mouth is so dry that I can hardly even croak. I sense her settling down beside the box, keeping me company, but after a while even she pads away. I guess it's too hot for her.

Someone will come and let me out soon, won't they?

I wonder where Daddy is? But it wouldn't matter even if he knew where I was. He isn't kind to me; everybody thinks I'm not really his daughter, and I think that's why they don't like me. *Oh, let me out. Please come and let me out.*

I hear Auntie Cyn yelling at the kids to get to bed, and my brother and sister squabbling over who gets to sleep in the tent tonight. Somebody gets the belt for being sassy to Grandma. Eventually they start calling out 'Goodnight'.

One of my little cousins says, 'Where's Ame?' But I don't hear the answer.

Is someone going to come for me?

It's gotten real quiet outside now.

Mommy. I'll think about Mommy. And the times with her and my other Daddy, when we lived in an apartment in Pennsylvania. He said he loved to hear me giggle, and sing.

Oh, I can't breathe.

Mommy and Kenneth got me the karaoke machine so I could sing all the time, and we had so much fun. We laughed at Kenneth because he thought he was a great singer, but he really wasn't!

I've had to go to the toilet in here and it smells so bad.

When they taught me to ride my bike, I was so frightened of falling off at first, and I clung onto Mommy all the way round the park. And then Mommy told me I was a brave girl and I could do it by myself, and so I let go and Mommy was so proud of me.

Mommy, you were proud of me, weren't you?

And I used to help Mommy bake cakes and we made a special one for a birthday. Whose birthday was it?

I need to get out. I need to get out.

I wonder what Mommy's doing now?

Please, please let me out. I'm suffocating.

I once used to play with my sister and her doll. What was her name? Blondie? Brandie?

Breathe in, breathe out. They'll come soon. Won't they?

An Overview of Ame's Case

Ame Deal
24.07.00 – 12.07.11
aged 10 years & 11 months
Phoenix, Arizona

On the morning of 12 July 2011, Officer Albert Salaiz responded to a call about an injured child at a property in a rundown neighbourhood of Phoenix, Arizona. As he approached, he recalled that he had visited the home only a few days earlier, in response to a call about kids throwing rocks.

The officer found a small child, curled up on a towel, knees to her chest and with 'claw-like hands'. He knew that she was dead. There was a footlocker nearby.

The family claimed that while the adults had been asleep the previous night, some of the children had been playing hide-and-seek, and Ame had climbed into one of her favourite hiding places, and accidentally locked herself in. In parrot fashion, the children repeated this story.

But it was soon to be revealed that this was completely untrue, and that the little girl who had endured years of abuse by multiple family members, had died a horrific death on that hot July night.

Ame Lynn Deal was born in Monongahela, Pennsylvania, to Shirley, who was married to David Deal at the time, and with whom she had two children. The identity of Ame's birth father is in doubt, as although David's name is on the birth certificate, Shirley was in a relationship with a man named Kenneth Griest, with whom she and her children lived for the first three or four years of Ame's life.

When Ame was somewhere between four and seven years old, Shirley claims that she was intimidated by her husband, David Deal, to move into his family's residence, in Midland, Texas. The adults in the home included David's mother, Judith Deal, and his sister, Cynthia Stoltzmann. Shirley said that she, but not the children, were abused during the two years she lived there, and that she was 'kicked out of the house' and fled, without her children, hoping to get them back some day.

Between 1988 and 2010, the Deal-Stoltzmann clan moved 28 times across New Mexico, Wisconsin, Texas, Pennsylvania, and Utah. During the time of their residence in Ogden, Utah, Ame attended school, where staff reported evidence of abuse to the DCFS at least three times. Court records indicate that Ame was listed as an "abused, neglected child". She was not however, removed from the home for her protection.

It is my understanding that family or other witnesses also called Child Protection, believing that Ame would be "rescued and put with a good family". One particular witness was in despair when she learned that the family had fled once again.

Eventually, they settled into a squalid property in a poor neighbourhood of Phoenix, Arizona. The residence was home to several adults and children, some of whom lived in tents erected in the back yard. Once settled in Phoenix, with the children allegedly being homeschooled, there was no contact with any authorities who might have raised red flags.

Ame's aunt Cynthia was her official guardian, and her father, who did not reside there all the time, always doubted her paternity. This seems to have made Ame the scapegoat of the entire family. Cynthia's daughter, Sammantha and her husband John Allen, and their four children also lived in the home. daughter.

This diagram shows the members of the Deal-Stoltzmann family who were the main perpetrators of Ame's torture.

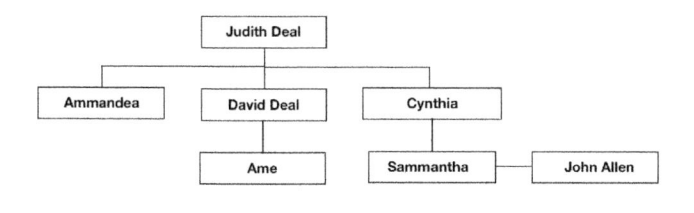

```
                        Judith Deal
                             │
        ┌────────────────────┼────────────────────┐
   Ammandea            David Deal              Cynthia
                             │                     │
                            Ame              Sammantha ── John Allen
```

The matriarch is Judith Deal: Ammandea, David and Cynthia are her children.
Cynthia Stoltzmann was Ame's legal guardian.
Sammantha is Cynthia's daughter, and her husband is John Allen.
The Allens had four children, and Ame had several siblings and half-siblings.

Neighbours later reported that they had frequently seen and heard the adults yelling at the children, who would play outside as late as 2am. They witnessed Ame being forced to walk up and down the sidewalk in bare feet in temperatures of 114 degrees.

Ame was beaten with a wooden paddle, named the Butt Buster, lashed with a belt, fed hot sauce, chained up like a dog, and forced to eat dog faeces. Her bedroom was an empty shower stall, with no pillow or blanket. Cynthia was heard by neighbours to scream at and beat Ame for having "wetted herself". Again, the cycle of fear, bathroom accidents, more fear.

But it was the punishment of the footlocker that must have terrified the quiet and polite little girl the most.

Crammed into an area far too small for her frame, she would be made to spend hours in the suffocating space. The only way that air could get into the box was via tiny holes beneath the handles. Crying to be let out brought no respite; her own father threw the box into the pool when her pleading got on his nerves. Various family members would spin and throw the box around. And her aunt Cynthia would sit her full weight upon it and tap away on her laptop.

Despite the story told by the whole family that Ame had locked herself in the foot locker during a game of hide-and-seek, it was found on examination that it was not possible to lock the box from the inside. Ame's uncle, John Allen, then said that his three-year-old daughter must have padlocked the box. Under questioning, John Allen changed his story several times, and with the hide-and-seek story in tatters, when left alone in an interview room with his wife, he incriminated himself and others, saying: "We should have come up with something very solid, all together as a family, and nobody would have to take the fall."

Allen later admitted when questioned that he had locked Ame into the box that night, thrown it around, and that he had done so on previous occasions. He also admitted to taking the key with him and hiding the lock. In the over

95 degree heat of an Arizona July night, Ame was locked inside a plastic box in a sweltering garage.

Allen's confession led to the arrests of other adults in the family.

Judith Deal, the matriarch of the brood, was charged with kidnapping and child abuse, and sentenced to ten years, and it seems she was released in February 2020, with a lifetime of probation.

Her daughter, Cynthia Stoltzmann, was also charged with kidnapping and child abuse, and sentenced to 24 years, and lifetime probation.

As the perpetrators of that particular evening's torture, Cynthia's daughter, Sammantha, and her husband, John Allen, were charged with murder in the first degree, numerous acts of child abuse, and conspiracy to commit child abuse. Sammantha's defence team claimed that her upbringing and loyalty to her mother gave her no other frame of reference than the world of filth and abuse she had lived in her entire life. This did not spare her the death sentence that she and her husband were handed down. They have the distinction of being the first married couple to be sentenced to death in Arizona.

Ammandea Stoltzmann, another of Judith Deal's daughters, and Ame's aunt, was also arrested on three counts of felony abuse, which took place when she had lived with the rest of the family in Texas. The 24-year-old admitted that she had hit Ame, kept her chained up outside overnight wearing a dog collar, and forced her to drink hot sauce so strong that it made her own eyes water and burn just being near it. The charges were later dropped.

Ame's 'father' David Deal, who admitted one day throwing the plastic box that Ame was confined to into the pool, because she was crying that she couldn't breathe, pleaded guilty to attempted child abuse and possession of marijuana, and was handed down a 14-year-sentence.

Ame's autopsy revealed that she had died from asphyxiation, compounded by heat exhaustion and dehydration. At the time of her death, a few days shy of her 11th birthday, Ame was just four feet two inches tall, and she weighed only 59 lbs (26.76 kg). The average weight for her age is 81.5 lbs (36.97 kg).

It remains unclear whether Ame had been permitted to take a popsicle that afternoon in the 100 degree heat, along with the other children, or whether she had committed the heinous crime of taking one without permission.

I will end this heart-wrenching tale with the words of my fellow advocate against child murder by abuse, Laine, of the Suffer The Little Children podcast and blog:

> "This slow, horrific, unimaginable manner of death–this brutal murder–was forced upon a sweet, innocent, ten-year-old girl, just because she ate a popsicle on a hot Arizona evening. If that's not enough to crush your heart to a pulp, you may want to make sure you have one."

My grateful thanks to my reader, Sharon J, from Phoenix, Arizona, for alerting me to Ame's story

Rest Safely in Peace, Ame

Abusive Families

Whilst all of my books concern assaults and torture within the family, it is often just one or two perpetrators who commit the abuse. But as I research more and more 'abused to death' cases, I am shocked to see how many involve three or more abusers.

I like to hope that Ame had someone in the home who was kind to her, but by and large, it seems the entire family was at the very least complicit, and in many cases active, in her torture. When the whole family colludes against a scapegoat, the child has no respite from both mental and physical suffering.

Perhaps it should be no surprise, in a way, because we know that children learn from those around them, and some may know nothing but violence and depravity within their family.

In the Deal-Stoltzman trials, Sammantha's defence put forward that she had no knowledge outside her upbringing of filth and abuse. She had only reached fourth grade at school.

Her husband, John Allen, was the only one outside the blood descendants of Judith Deal to be indicted for the abuse of Ame. Was he already pre-disposed to the levels of cruelty that made him padlock a child into a plastic box? Or was he totally brainwashed by living with the Deal family?

My research has taken this concept a stage further.

I have found that when two of these abusive families come together, perhaps by marriage, they add up to more than the sum of their parts, having much more than double the capacity for cruelty. Once each family finds their own level of depravity accepted, and duly accepts the torture carried out by the other family, they create a toxic eruption that spews down upon an innocent child (or children).

A case in point is the family dynamic that existed in the home of Baby Brianna Lopez. Both the maternal and paternal sides of family participated in the hideous abuse of the five-month-old baby. (If you'd like to join my Readers' Team, you can pick up your free ebook, in which I cover this case.) The two main perpetrators were from opposite 'sides' of the family; her birth father, and her maternal uncle, with the abuse seemingly tolerated and accepted by the various other family members who lived in the home.

In another example, reflecting on the 'monsters' that British serial killers Fred and Rose West became, we cannot ignore that their childhoods were built on incest and rage. I imagine that when they met each other as adults, they may have at first tested the waters a little, to see if certain words and behaviours were shocking to their other half, and when accepted and encouraged, they each felt they had been given the green light, after which their cruelty knew no bounds.

But some family members escape this prison of depravity, and I repeat this in all my books:

Whilst abusers were often abused as children

All abused children do not become abusers

There will be exceptions to the first of these statements, and I would not wish to offend the family of a person who turns out to be an abuser, because other factors do come into play, such as the strong influence of a partner, drug abuse, psychiatric illnesses, etc.

And regarding the second statement; abused children who break out of the horrific bonds that could have enslaved them in to continuing the cycle: You are heroes. You are saving lives every day.

The Perfect Mother

Lois lies in bed, staring at the ceiling, with her husband snoring beside her. She clutches at the sheets.

Dear Lord, give me the strength to do what I have to do this night.

Harold stirs. Turns over. Goes back to sleep.

She smiles in the darkness. He's a good man. Hard working, and brings in the money to allow her to run her beautiful home. She loves him for that. Thinking about her husband soothes her mind for a while, until the thoughts are back.

What do you want of me, Lord? What more can I do?

If only Dennis was more like Roddy, there would be no need for any of it. Roddy had only needed to spend a few minutes here and there kneeling on the broomstick, and then he could say his catechism faster than any of her friends' children.

And if only Dennis hadn't been so darn chubby. And with that smile. That's not how children should be. With all that energy! Like a wild beast. Roddy had stood exactly where she told him, and spoken only when spoken to, right from the start.

Why did you send Dennis to me, Lord?

It's to test her faith. She knows that deep inside. But she wishes the test wasn't so difficult. What child has such an ugly belly button, for goodness sake! At least he's not quite as fat as he was when he came, but she can still pinch his side and grab more flesh than she would like to.

And then there's the other thing. The disgusting, filthy wetting of the bed. Roddy was potty-trained long before this. But not Dennis, oh no!

Lord, do you want me to go now and check him?

She gently pulls back the covers. Harold grunts. She waits. Then she tiptoes down the hall.

Roddy sleeps with one eye half-open. 'Shh, can't you, Dennis?'

Dennis murmurs something he can't quite hear, and sobs again.

Roddy sighs. 'Don't cry. Come on, try and get some sleep now.'

'Can't sleep. She come.'

'Try, Dennis. She might not come tonight.'

Dennis whimpers.

'It's Sunday tomorrow. Our best day. We've got new shirts to wear.'

Dennis is calming down; maybe there'll be peace tonight. Roddy tries to believe that if he can keep him calm, nothing bad will happen. Sometimes he's right.

He waits a few minutes. 'You asleep now?' he whispers.

No reply. The whole house seems quiet at last.

Lois hesitates outside the door.

Give me the strength to do Your holy work. Give me courage, Lord. Don't leave me.'

But she can sense Him slipping away.

He often deserts her, when she gets close to it. Testing her. She tries her best to please Him, but it's never enough. She will try harder tonight.

She thinks of Dennis on the other side of the door. Pudgy and stupid. That big fat face. She chuckles to herself. Not quite so fat now.

But he'll be all wet and ugly and she'll have to try hard to do God's work.

Come back, Lord. Help me.

She turns the handle. Slowly, quietly.

Roddy is awake, so she smiles and presses her finger to her lips. 'Shh, my darling.'

'Mama, please don't,' he whispers. But he knows it's no good.

'You're a good boy, Roddy. But I have to do it. You know I have to.'

She approaches Dennis' bed. She knew it. She just knew it.

'You filthy boy!' she yells. 'Why can't you obey your mama?'

Dennis screams.

'He can't help it, Mama,' says Roddy.

But she doesn't hear anything. God has truly deserted her now, and it's just her and the fat, ugly child on the bed, soaked in his own waste.

She towers over him. 'I will make you stop!'

Dennis screams again as she punches him with a powerful fist. He squeezes his eyes shut. But she slaps his face until he opens them again, her contorted features an inch from his nose.

'Mama, please,' says Roddy, but his voice is just a faint whisper. He looks across at his little brother, willing him not to do it again. That thing he shouldn't do.

But his mother's booming voice tells him that Dennis couldn't hold it in.

Don't bite it, Mama. Please don't bite it.

Their mother fumbles in her pocket for a clothes pin. 'Let's see if this'll stop you, you dirty, disgusting boy!'

Dennis yelps as she snaps it onto his penis.

Roddy lies still, sweat pouring onto his sheets.

Mama has the belt ready and it whips through the air. Roddy stops counting after ten lashes. Then, with a final punch to Dennis' face, it's over.

'Goodnight, my good son,' she says to Roddy, as she leaves the room.

'You did it, didn't you?'

Dennis can barely speak for sobbing. 'Can't stop it.'

'You gotta squeeze and keep it in, like I do.'

'Won't stay in.'

'I'll try to show you how again tomorrow, okay?'

'Okay.' That catch in his throat. Trying to be brave.

'Hey, you know what? I don't think Mama will come back tonight.'

Dennis gives a hopeless, disbelieving sigh.

Even if she doesn't come again tonight, she'll be back tomorrow, all day, and the next day, and the day after that. They can't remember a day since Dennis came that she hasn't spent most of it torturing him.

Back in her own room, Lois thanks God for His guidance, and prays for more strength to discipline her wayward boy again tomorrow.

Sundays are different to all the other days. The boys get their hair slicked down and in their white shirts and blue shorts and shiny shoes, and with Dennis wearing sunglasses, they take their parents' hands and go to church. Two whole hours when Mama won't be punching or biting or scalding. When she isn't looking, Papa helps Dennis with his prayer book, nodding as the little boy does his best to say the words he's tried to learn by heart. When Mama notices, she glares at her husband.

'Lovely service,' say Mama and Papa, on their way out into the heat of the day.

The minister smiles. 'Those boys sure are growing, Mrs Jurgens, Mr Jurgens.'

'They can be a heap of trouble, but it's worth it to know we're guiding them the right way.'

'Well, they're a credit to you, Ma'am.'

Mama is almost blushing as she leads the way over to her friends.

'You're so good to give those two little orphan boys a nice, clean home, Lois,' says Mrs Hogan.

'Just doing the Lord's Will,' says Mama. 'He gives me all the strength I need, especially when Dennis is a bad boy and has to be punished.'

Mama's friends smile down at Roddy and scowl at Dennis.

'Well, I know I couldn't do it,' says Mrs Beech. 'Why'd you take the other one in, when you already had this fine boy?' She ruffles Roddy's hair.

'I sometimes wonder, Mrs Beech. But you know, in some ways it's not his fault. His Mama was no good.'

The friends nod.

'And I'd take in more poor little children if I could,' says Lois, puffing up her chest like she's the perfect mother. 'If that's what the Good Lord has planned for me. Dennis!'

The three-year-old starts. 'Yes, Mama?'

'What did I tell you about keeping your hair neat?'

'I'm sorry, Mama.'

'You will be, boy.'

'Don't be too hard on him, Lois,' says Mrs Wood. 'It's the heat. Look at all the other kids. My Tommy's hair's all over the place!'

'Dennis' is worse,' snaps Mama. 'I'll see to him at home.'

Mrs Wood and Mrs Fleming exchange glances.

'Should I repeat my new bible verses, Mama?' says Roddy, hoping to delay their return to the house.

'Did you ever know such a good boy!' says Lois, smiling at him, before turning proudly to her friends again. 'Just a few verses, and then we'll get back.'

After the first few lines, Roddy's plan to help his brother backfires.

'Join in, Sloppy-Fat,' says Mama. 'Recite the bible with Roddy, like a good boy.'

Dennis mouths the words the best he can, but Lois howls with laughter.

'Useless! That's another punishment for you, my boy!'

Mrs Wood tries again. 'He's just a baby, Lois. He'll learn them soon.'

Mama rounds on her. 'You may think that's good enough for your offspring, Adelaide, but *my* children better know their bible inside out by now.'

Roddy squeezes his brother's hand, following their mother as she stalks away. Their palms are sticky, and they wipe them on their shorts, hoping Mama won't notice later that they got their Sunday clothes all mussed up.

The effort of holding back for those two whole hours must've been unbearable for their mother, because as soon as they're shut behind that door again, Dennis is thrown down the stairs and whipped with the belt, with Mama calling out, 'I'm doing this for you, boy. I'm just doing God's Holy Work.'

And Papa's already out back, tinkering with that old car of his.

Roddy can't remember much of how it was before Dennis came. He was always scared of Mama's temper, of course. But he doesn't recall too many beatings back then. Mama has always called him her good boy, which he guesses is because he's quiet, and right from the beginning, he didn't soil himself or his diaper more than she allowed. And because he'd potty trained pretty easy, she never became obsessed with his pecker or his toilet habits.

But it wasn't long after Dennis arrived that Roddy saw her hold him down and pour boiling water on his little pee-pee. His screams were a mixture of agony and shock. At that time, they weren't tied down on opposite sides of the room, so when she threw him back onto the bed frame, Roddy could creep out of his own bed and cuddle his new little brother, and try to teach him how to hold it in. Dennis couldn't do it though. He was just a baby after all. When she started putting the metal clothes pin on the end of it at night, and tied him to the frame, he'd cry and say, 'Off, Roddy,' and he'd take it off for as long as he dared.

Once, when she was biting it, saying, 'Let's just get rid of it, dirty little thing,' Dennis couldn't hold on and peed right into her mouth. She broke his arm dragging him off the bed and out of the room, out of Roddy's sight. Roddy had put his hands over his ears but he couldn't shut it out; the thud of her kicks, his pitiful moaning, her rippling laughter.

Roddy has a hazy recollection of his real mom and dad, but he feels sure they were nice to him, and they just had some problems which meant they couldn't keep him. His grandparents took care of him for a time too, which was pretty neat. But they've both been told that Dennis' mama was a bad girl who didn't obey the Lord. He does wonder though, whether a bad girl would've bashed her child's head against a nail she'd hammered into the wall.

There's a beautiful photograph of Dennis and Roddy, taken one Sunday, before Dennis got too many bruises, and had to wear sunglasses to church. They look like a pair of cherubs; those sweet chubby angels you see in Mama's books. But when Mama saw the photo, she started calling Dennis a fat sloppy pig, and cutting his food down even more. And the food he was allowed to have didn't look good, especially when Mama spread it an inch thick with horseradish sauce. She forced him to eat it as he flushed up and tears streamed down his face. When he tried to spit it out she put her hands over his mouth and nose to make it go down, and Dennis went purple and his chest heaved. When he threw it up, she made him eat that too.

The boys have to say their Rosary every night. Roddy was quick to learn and could reel off the prayers without a hitch by the time he was two.

But Dennis was just a baby, and terrified of their mama, and he would trip over the words time and again. Mama thought it was a good idea to make him kneel on a broomstick and say it over and over till he got it right. Roddy had to do it himself once or twice. Boy, did that hurt.

Just now and then, there are happy days. Roddy still gets to see his real grandma sometimes, and when Mama gets sick and Papa has to go to work, he and Dennis get driven in Grandma's old pickup to her house on the edge of town, near the lake. Dennis doesn't speak at first, and keeps looking over his shoulder, waiting for someone to come and destroy the dream.

'What you crying for, little man?' asks Grandma, soon after they arrive.

'No, no,' he whimpers.

'You hurt, Dennis?'

'No, Ma'am.'

'Grandma,' says Roddy. 'He cries when he wets his diaper. He knows he's gonna get punished.'

'Oh, you poor child,' says Grandma. 'Who cares about an old wet diaper? You come to Grandma and we'll get that changed lickety-split.'

Dennis shrinks back from her arms. He's seen his mama play this game.

'Grandma won't hurt you, Dennis,' says Roddy.

Grandma picks him up and cuddles him into her, not caring that the sodden terry-towel is wetting her lap. 'Come on now, honey,' she whispers. 'Let's get you nice and dry so you can go play with your brother.'

That first day they get candy to eat and watch cartoons on TV, but Dennis always makes sure Roddy is positioned between him and Grandma. Towards the end of the week though, Roddy sees his brother smile; he hasn't seen that in a while. Dennis even starts to copy Roddy and clamber up onto Grandma's knee, and they take turns at Grandma's 'Cuddle Factory'.

'Just can't stop making these pesky cuddles, boys. Somebody better climb up and take some real quick before they disappear.'

Dennis squeals with delight as the old woman holds him in her arms and tickles his tummy, saying, 'This here spot needs a little more candy, don't you think?'

'We live with you now, Grandma?' says Dennis one day. He doesn't notice her hesitation.

'For now you do, honey. For now you're my boys.'

He beams and hugs her, and Grandma shushes Roddy as he starts to tell him that 'For now' means they have to go back home sometime.

They have six wonderful weeks.

After that, Roddy hears his grandma talking on the phone. 'Just you take your time, Lois. Make sure you're better before you … Yes, yes I understand that, but you must be tired. I can keep them till … Then let me take them a couple of days every week. They're such sweet boys. I'd like to see them growing. I could help you out and ... Alright, okay, six o'clock.'

Mama screeches with laughter when she sees them. 'Mercy, woman! You been fattening my boys up like Thanksgiving turkeys!'

Dennis is white-faced and silent.

'Come to Mama, Mr Sloppy-Fat.'

Dennis scoots round behind Grandma's skirts. Roddy stands beside him and takes his hand. A puddle glimmers on the tiled floor and a wet stain blooms on Dennis' shorts.

Grandma turns to pick him up. 'Oh honey, you had a little accident. But it's okay. He's been dry for three weeks, Lois. I'm sorry, I should've put a diaper on.'

'Now, don't you worry about that. I'll sort him out quick-smart. Give him to me.' She smiles coldly at Dennis as Grandma passes him over.

Dennis stiffens and doesn't say a word.

'Bye bye, Grandma,' whispers Roddy, and hugs her legs.

'I'll keep that old Cuddle Factory working,' she murmurs into his hair. 'Mind you tell Dennis that.'

He tells him that night as his little brother lies strapped to the bed, naked but for the clothes peg clipped onto the end of his penis. He doesn't even smile.

They both lose the few pounds they'd gained pretty quickly, but Dennis doesn't lose it fast enough for Mama's liking.

'Think you can go and get all fat and sloppy behind my back?' She lashes Dennis with the belt. 'And ugly! You've gotten real ugly again, Mister. That tummy button just about makes me sick.' More lashes. 'I can't look at that fat, ugly face another second. So get your sorry butt outside and wait till I tell you to come back in.'

Dennis starts to pick up his shoes.

'Did I say you could wear shoes? Did I?'

'No, Mama.'

'I can't hear you.'

'No, Mama.'

'So get out there and stand out back till I fetch you.'

'Mama.' Roddy tugs on her sleeve. 'Mama, the snow. It's real deep out back.'

'You questioning your mama, Roddy? You want to stand outside with your sloppy-fat brother?'

'I guess not, Mama.'

Lois pats his head. 'Dear Lord, help this poor child so he won't go the same way as his no-good brother.'

Dennis is still at the door, transfixed.

'Get out of my sight,' says Mama, hurling a shoe at his face.

'Now, Roddy. Let me hear you say the Rosary. Make us both feel a whole lot better.'

Mrs Wood and Mrs Fleming stand in the doorway. 'We heard you were organising the Easter flowers this year, Lois. Wondered if you might need a hand.'

'Well, you heard that wrong, Ladies. I'm far too busy these days with that boy!'

'Oh, Lois, we'd sure love to see them both. We haven't seen little Dennis in church for some while now.'

Why can't they keep their noses out of other people's business?

'He's resting right now, Adelaide. Didn't sleep too good last night. But Roddy's here. Roddy, sweetheart, come and say Hi to Mama's friends.'

Roddy approaches the door, hanging back just enough so that the ladies might step inside to ruffle his hair or pinch his cheek, and see Dennis, slumped on the chair, pale and lifeless.

'Isn't he a fine boy?' says Lois. 'Smartest boy in town. Say your Rosary for Mrs Wood, Roddy.'

'I–I can't think of it, Mama.'

Lois howls with laughter, but Roddy feels her nails digging into his arm. 'Oh, my Lord. You sure know how to tease your mama.'

'It's alright, Lois,' says Mrs Fleming. 'We just wanted to drop by and see if we could help with the flowers. We'll be getting along now.'

'But you didn't hear Roddy recite his prayers for you …'

'See you Sunday, Mrs Jurgens.'

Lois slams the door and whirls on Roddy. 'You can't remember the Rosary? All of a sudden, when my friends are here, you can't remember the Virgin Mary's prayers?'

'I'm sorry, Mama. I don't know what happened.'

'Fetch the broom, Roddy.'

'I'm sorry, Mama.'

'Fetch it.'

He kneels down on the broom, ready to recite.

Mama pushes him down the broom towards the head. 'Dennis, get up on here.'

'But Mama, it was me,' says Roddy. 'Dennis didn't do anything bad this time.'

'Don't you try to protect him, son. Don't let him teach you his bad ways. Dennis, get on the broom, and say your prayers with your brother. And you'd better get every word right.'

Within a few weeks, Dennis is nothing but skin and bone. Mama spends a lot of time doing 'God's Work' on him, and Roddy is told to keep out of the way. When he hears his little brother go crashing down the stairs again, he creeps to the bedroom door to see Mama clattering down after him, cursing. Roddy steals along the landing and peeps out through the rail. Mama is kicking Dennis in the stomach, and he's stopped screaming. As she raises her knee, ready to stomp even harder, Roddy scrambles down the steps. 'Stop it, Mama! Please stop!'

'Get back in your room. Now, Roddy.'

Dennis' eyes are rolling around in his head.

'Please, Mama.'

'Now, Roddy!'

He races back upstairs, heading for Mama and Papa's room. Where could Papa be? Maybe this time, if he sees it happening, he'll speak up and help Dennis. But Papa is not at home, and Mama is on her way back up, dragging Dennis by his arm. He's flopping like a rag doll.

'That's right, Roddy. You be a good boy and go and wait in Mama's room while I attend to this dirty dog. Dear Lord, you sure make me work hard to save this boy's soul.'

That night, Dennis screams as Mama throws him onto his bed.

Roddy peeps over his blanket. 'Mama, is he okay?'

'He'll be fine, son. Don't you be worrying about *him*.' She turns to Dennis. 'Quit that howling. You'll keep your brother awake.'

When Mama has gone, Roddy creeps across the room. 'Dennis, Dennis?'

The younger boy screams again at Roddy's gentle touch.

'I'm sorry, Dennis. What can I do?'

Dennis lies still, moaning pitifully.

'Remember the Cuddle Factory, Dennis? Remember how we climbed up on Grandma's knee and she squeezed us real tight. You remember that, Dennis?' Roddy wants to cry, but he tries to be brave for his little brother. 'I bet Grandma will come for us soon and we can go there. How'd that be, Dennis? Wouldn't that be great?'

But Dennis' eyes have glazed over. He doesn't hear a word.

An Overview of Dennis' Case

Dennis Craig Jurgens
aged 3 years and 4 months
06.12.61 – 11.04.65
Minnesota, USA

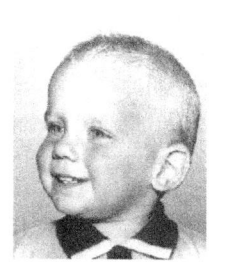

Dennis Craig Puckett was born to a teenage mother who was a ward of court. In those days, young, unmarried mothers were not viewed as suitable parents, and Jerry Sherwood was urged to give up her baby.

Waiting in the wings, were Harold and Lois Jurgens, a church-going couple who were unable to have children of their own, and Harold's job as an electrical foreman afforded the couple a comfortable home in White Bear Lake, Minnesota.

Dennis' birth mother may have been young and inexperienced, but the woman he was placed with turned out to be a psychopathic killer.

One of 16 children born into a family scarred by alcohol abuse, Lois had had a difficult childhood, but as a respectable married woman, she was determined to present an affluent front to her friends and neighbours. Due to her psychiatric problems, which included mania and uncontrollable rage, for which she had undergone the now less commonly utilised electric shock treatment, the couple had previously been told by state agencies that they were unsuitable candidates to become adoptive parents.

Undeterred however, they privately adopted a boy (who I have called Roddy in my story). This presumably demonstrated that they were suitable after all, and deciding they wanted another child, the process of adopting Dennis Puckett was initiated.

Despite the glowing report from their Catholic priest that they were ideal parents to adopt a second child, at the initial meeting of Dennis and the Jurgens', the social worker had reservations about placing the energetic, fun-loving one-year-old with the obsessively clean and regimental Lois. The prospective mother described the friendly child with the beaming smile as 'awful looking' and 'disobedient', but with few alternatives available to the Jurgens', and the agency unable to give a definitive reason against the match, the adoption went ahead.

Lois' antipathy towards the child was clear from the start, with her giving him the nickname 'Sloppy-Fat' whilst referring to Roddy as 'my good son'. The chief misdemeanour of this baby seems to have been that he didn't potty train as quickly as Lois demanded. This was the catalyst for the numerous punishments he endured during his short life.

Lois Jurgens had wanted the perfect family, and she sought admiration for the domestic life she tried to create. She kept her house and garden in immaculate order, and demanded that her adopted children were clean, quiet and obedient. Unfortunately, Dennis was more lively than she wanted him to be, and had a mind of his own, and Lois turned against him with increasing levels of cruelty.

Within a few months, Dennis was taken to the local hospital with burns to his stomach, buttocks and genitals. Although the doctor felt the injuries were strange, he accepted Lois' explanation that she had accidentally turned the bath water on too high. In addition to scalding, Dennis was subjected to lifting up by the ears, various forms of battery, having a clothes pin (clothes peg in the UK) attached to his penis, kneeling on a broomstick to recite prayers, being bitten on his penis and scrotum, being tied to the toilet until he had a bowel movement, and bound to the bed.

The energetic little boy was gradually reduced to a bruised, pitifully thin husk; a world away from the smiling cherub seen in photographs before he fell into Lois' hands. From the age of one to three and a half, while under the Jurgens' 'care', his weight increased by only three pounds. At his death, he had little or no subcutaneous fat and 50–100 injuries.

Dennis died of peritonitis, his small bowel having been perforated through blunt force trauma (likely through kicking), and its contents leaking into his abdominal cavity, causing hours or days of agonising pain. Multiple lacerations and bruises were also found on his body. It was later, much later, concluded that his fatal injuries could not have been caused by a fall, but bringing Dennis' murderer to justice took many years.

In 1965, little was known about the potential of a parent to murder their own child; it was beyond most people's understanding. However, the coroner who examined Dennis' body, Dr Votel, reported that he believed Dennis was a 'battered child' and on being told the death was being investigated by the police, he marked the file as 'deferred' pending the outcome. But Dennis' case slipped through the net. Lois' younger brother, Jerome Zerwas, was a lieutenant on the local police force, and many people suspected that he played a role in covering up his sister's crime.

There was, however, enough concern to instigate a hearing in the juvenile court, with approximately 50 friends, relations and neighbours testifying to the sadistic abuse they had witnessed. This resulted in Roddy being removed from his adoptive parents, but no charges were brought against Lois Jurgens. The record of the investigation was sealed, and Dennis was buried.

Roddy was placed with his own family members and a foster family. During the time he was living with his grandparents, Roddy was in hospital with pneumonia when his grandmother was burned to death in a house fire at her home. Lois Jurgens had threatened many times to burn down the houses of neighbours and relatives who had spoken up about her behaviour, but she was not charged with arson. She spent a great deal of time and money trying to get Roddy back, and with his grandmother out of the picture, Lois got her way, albeit a few years later.

In addition to Roddy, the Jurgens' were permitted to adopt more children, and Lois resumed her sadistic behaviour upon four siblings from Kentucky. She was reported to have instructed her husband Harold to also beat the children, but instead he took them down to the basement and told them to scream as if in pain.

The children were all of school age, and were later able to describe the abuse in the family home. All five children managed to escape and get help, and another juvenile hearing was launched, with social worker Carol Felix being given permission to open the previously sealed file. Upon reading it, she became convinced that Dennis had been abused and murdered, but her efforts to re-open the case were unsuccessful. The Jurgens' were simply banned from fostering or adopting any more children.

In 1981, discovering the surname of Dennis' adoptive parents, his birth mother, Jerry Sherwood, began to search for her first-born son. Jerry had remained with Dennis' father for many years, and they had four more children together. As Dennis would now be a young man, Jerry thought he might like to have the chance to meet his siblings.

At first, she found old newspaper clippings reporting that Dennis had died of peritonitis 16 years earlier. After a further five years had passed, Jerry decided to resume her enquiries. When she located Dennis' death certificate with its wording 'deferred', Jerry investigated further, taking her case to the police and the media, and was horrified to read the evidence of her baby's probable torture in the 21-year-old file. Dennis' body was exhumed and, it being remarkably well preserved, it confirmed the three-year-old's many injuries.

Jerry Sherwood's tenacity to find justice for her son paid off, and Lois Jurgens was put on trial. The key witness was Roddy, Dennis' older brother. Only five at the time of Dennis' death, he was powerless to prevent the torture, but his testimony at Jurgens' trial ensured that his adoptive mother was convicted. The four siblings from Kentucky also spoke of daily beatings, and other abuse, such as slamming a child's forehead into a nail hammered into a wall, being made to stand barefoot in the snow, and having a used sanitary napkin pushed into the face.

Lois Jurgens was ultimately convicted of third-degree murder and served only eight years in prison. She died, proclaiming her innocence, in 2013, at the age of 87.

A Death in White Bear Lake, a true crime book by Barry Siegel (Bantam, June 1990) tells Dennis' story, highlighting the mistakes made at the time of his death.

Famous Crimes of Minnesota by Michael Burgan (Adventure Publications, July 2013) also gives further details about the case.

A 1992 NBC television film named A Child Lost Forever, starring Beverly D'Angelo, tells the story from Dennis' birth mother, Jerry Sherwood's perspective.

Rest Safely in Peace, Dennis

Bodily Functions

An abusive parent frequently 'disciplines' a child due to bathroom accidents. And that 'discipline' can lead to murder.

Lois Jurgens is a case in point. Dennis was a cheerful and lively one-year-old when he fell into her clutches. But any skills he may have begun to acquire in controlling his bladder and bowels were erased by her incandescent rages, and her cruel and ludicrous methods of potty-training.

As this occurs with such sickening frequency, I have given this a great deal of thought. How on earth do we resolve this, and end such practices as tying a small child to a bed-frame with a clothes-pin on his penis?

Midwives, health visitors, and other medical personnel offer parenting skills, such as feeding, and how to change a diaper. They are ideally placed to support new parents in various ways, and to stress even more emphatically, that urinating and defecating are natural bodily functions over which the baby has no control, and that they don't do these things to infuriate their parents.

Many diaper/nappy companies screen TV commercials show a gentle parent with a happy baby at changing time. But I feel they could incorporate two more things into these ads:

• Stress that the child is doing what comes naturally, and that kindness and patience will pay dividends

• Show a tired or mildly exasperated parent, so that parents can see that they're not alone in feeling that changing a diaper isn't always fun

With so many children being murdered by their parents for the 'crime' of doing something we all do, and over which a baby has little or no control, we need to explore all avenues to help parents view this for what it is; normal behaviour.

In the following stories, the murderers have disturbing fixations with their victim's genital areas, and accuse them of sexual conduct. I can only assume that as children themselves, they received confusing signals about sex and their own bodies, where boundaries were crossed, leading to disastrous consequences for those now in their power.

The case of Poppie, coming next in this book, captures that perfectly, when the mother of the two children, aged three and five, accuses them of "wanting to fuck each other". We have to wonder where that alarming question springs from.

The last case is that of Takoda, whose father also focuses on his son's private parts as he administers horrific torture.

Invitation To My Readers' List

The children's stories continue in a moment, but first, I hope you'll be interested in this ...

If you share my passion to protect children, and would like to join my Readers' List, I'd love to welcome you by sending you a **FREE ebook**.

You will then gain access to **members only offers**, including the chance to receive an exclusive, **personally signed paperback book**, each new release at the subscriber price, special offers on similar books, and lots more.

Sound good?

Just pick up your free ebook and join us!

Details on the next page ...

Pick Up Your Free E-Book

Isaiah Torres was just six years old when he was abused to death in the most appalling way.

Don't miss this book, in which I also include bonus content about Baby Brianna Lopez.

Just scan this code:

Or use this link:

https://BookHip.com/KXACJDT

See overleaf to enter my draw ...

Enter My Draw

After you've joined us, I'll email you with an invitation to enter the draw for a members' exclusive **personally signed paperback book and bookmark**; UNIQUE only to winners of the draw.

Please don't miss the chance to enter, by being sure to check your Inbox, Junk or Spam, and you can also add my email address to your Contacts, and your safe sender / VIP list.

<u>jessicajackson@jesstruecrime.com</u>

(If you have problems signing up, just email me, and I'll be happy to add you manually.)

Good luck in the draw!

And by the way ...

Thanks To You

I donate royalties from my books to child protection charities – so far we've donated to: Prevent Child Abuse (US), NSPCC (UK) and UNICEF (worldwide).

I know that many of you will already be donating to children's charities yourselves, but I'd like to thank you for reading my books and helping me to protect children just a little more.

If you have any child protection charities to suggest, please just let me know.

Ready to carry on?

Playing Dead

As I pull the comb through the little girl's hair, another clump falls to the floor. 'Come on, Poppie,' I say. 'Hold your head up.'

'I'm tired,' she says.

'I know, baby, but I won't be able to get these tangles out if you keep drooping your head down.'

'I'm sorry, Breda.'

'Head up, Poppie!' growls Kobus from the other side of the room, and Poppie gets the strength from somewhere to raise her chin from her chest.

Still not satisfied, her stepfather heaves himself up from the chair and before I can help Poppie to move out of reach, he kicks her in the stomach.

Poppie yelps.

'Can't you leave her alone?' I say.

Kobus turns to me and scoffs, aiming a softer kick at my legs. He's never dared to treat me as badly as his own step-kids.

Poppie's pale skin has turned an even pastier shade, and I turn to my auntie for help. 'Look, Auntie. I don't think Poppie is feeling well.'

Aunt Louisa looks up from her magazine and starts to come over for a better look. A glare from Kobus stops her in her tracks. 'She's fine,' says Auntie. 'She always looks like that.'

I wasn't able to find a job after leaving school, so when my aunt Louisa and her husband Kobus said they needed help with their two little kids, and chores around the house, I jumped at the chance to move to Orania, up in the Northern Cape.

It's a pretty weird place though. Black people are banned from living and working here, and I miss the mixed cultures of my native city. Some folk call it 'the last outpost of apartheid'. But the people are friendly enough, I suppose. My aunt and her husband run a café in town, so they work hard and I guess they get tired after a long day.

My little cousins told me that their big sister used to look after them, but their stepfather kicked her out. Poppie and Joe miss her so much. But they've got used to me now, and I love taking care of them.

Kobus has given us permission to play in the park today, and the kids are running around with huge smiles on their faces. I've spent a little of my money on sweets too. I wave at Joe as he pushes his little sister on a swing. 'Don't go too high, Joey!'

'I won't, Breda!'

I realise that I'm seeing him play like a normal little boy for the first time in a long while. When an older boy goes up to the swings, I catch Joe pushing him out of the way. The bigger boy pushes him back of course, but Joe springs forward and kicks him in the shins.

'Joe, what are you doing? Let the other children take a turn!'

'Keep those kids under control, why don't you?' says a woman with frizzy blonde hair.

'I'm sorry. He's not usually like this. Come on, Joe. Play nicely and I'll get us all an ice-cream later.'

He shrugs, but helps his sister out of the swing, leaving it free for the other boy.

Poppie runs up and hugs me tightly. 'This is the best day of my life, Breda.'

I brush away a tear, and squeeze her as hard as I can. I feel her flinch, ever so slightly, and I remember her bruises. 'Sorry, sweetheart. Did I hurt you?'

'Oh, no! It's lovely.' She hugs me tighter.

'Want to go and play again?'

'Okay.' And she scoots off to join her brother on the slide.

'Be careful, you two!' But I'm smiling. It's wonderful to see them having fun like regular kids. I put my nose into my book for a moment, and when I look up again they're almost at the edge of the pond.

'Not too near the water, Joe!' I yell.

He turns and scowls at me; a look he's learnt from his stepfather. 'I can do what I want!'

'Not if it's dangerous! Come on, Joe. You'll fall in!'

'No! I won't. Stop telling me what to do!'

I realise that I don't know how to handle the kids if they're naughty. I've never had to do that before.

But Poppie bounds up with a huge smile and calls to her brother. 'Joey, it's time for our ice-creams!'

Poppie is lying on the mat before the fire.

'No, don't Kobus. Leave her, please,' says my aunt, but her husband barges past her and kicks Poppie right in the stomach. Again.

The tiny girl screams.

'I told you, Kobus. She's too tired today.'

'Not too tired to shit the fuckin' bed though, is she?' He kicks her again.

'Kobus! It's the phone call today!'

'She won't say anything,' he says. 'If she does, she knows what's coming.' He kicks again.

'Stop, Kobus. Please, stop!'

I've never seen my aunt so determined to protect her child. But of course, it's not out of love. It's so Poppie won't tell her real daddy.

Kobus gives my cousin a last kick before stalking out of the room.

Poppie turns onto her side to try and ease the pain.

I rage at my aunt. 'Look at her! God knows what damage he's doing to her and Joe! Why the hell don't you stop him?'

My aunt shrugs. 'Nothing much I can do. Anyway, she did shit the bed; she deserves it.'

'She deserves it? She's just a baby! And she's terrified of him. That's why she makes a mess. And Joe too.'

Aunt Louisa narrows her eyes at me before leaving the room. 'Watch your step, young lady.'

I join Poppie on the mat, where she's murmuring in her sweet little voice. I listen for a while and realise she's singing.

'Is that Hansie Slim?' I ask.

She nods. 'I'm practising for Pappa.'

'He likes that song, doesn't he?'

She smiles. 'My big sister taught me it.'

'She did, didn't she? And you sing it like a little angel.'

She reaches for me. I can tell every moment is agony for her.

'You want to sit on my knee?'

'Yes, please.'

I get up into a sitting position and gently lift her onto my lap.

'I miss her, Breda.'

'Who, baby?'

Her voice is so quiet I can hardly hear. 'Molly.'

'Your big sister. I know, baby, I know.'

'We used to play train-train.'

'You did? I bet that was fun.'

'Where did she go, Bre?'

'She went to go live with her own Pappa. It's a long way away.'

'Will you take me there?'

'Yes, Poppie. Yes, we'll go visit her when you're a bit older.'

'It's better to live with a real Pappa, isn't it, Bre?'

'Yes, sometimes.'

'They don't beat you.'

'No, honey. Pappas should never beat their children.' I hold her closer.

'It hurts, Breda.'

'I'm sorry, Poppie.'

'But we don't tell the teacher.'

I wish I knew what to do. 'Maybe *I* should tell the teacher.'

'No! I don't tell and you don't tell. But it hurts so bad.'

'I know, darling. Do you think we should tell your Pappa?'

'Oh no! Kobus will shout.'

I bury my face into her hair. 'Oh, baby, you're so brave.'

She's singing quietly again.

'It means Clever Hansel,' I say. Clever, like you!'

She smiles, but shakes her head. 'No, I'm stupid. Kobus says so.'

'No! You're clever and beautiful and brave.' I bend my head lower so she can't see my tears, and I hold her for a few more precious moments, until the phone rings.

'Poppie, are you ready? It's him,' yells Aunt Louisa. 'Five minutes.' She hands Poppie the phone.

Poppie starts to sing straight away, and I can hear her father gently laughing.

'Oh, Poppie, that's such a lovely song.'

'I practised for you, Pappa.'

'I can tell. You sang it perfectly. What a lucky Pappa I am.'

'We've been to the park.'

'You have? What did you do there?'

I love listening to Christo and Poppie's phone calls. Something bad must've happened to mean that he can't see the kids, but all I've ever heard in his voice is a father's love, pure and simple. I leave Poppie sitting on the floor and sink into a chair, and I can still hear Christo's warm, deep tone, and Poppie telling him about the slide and the swings, and then I guess he says something funny because she starts to giggle. Such a beautiful sound.

All too soon, Aunt Louisa is back. 'Give me that, Poppie.'

'Bye, Pappa.'

'Bye, sweetheart. Until next time. I love you to the moon and back.'

'To the moon and back,' says Poppie.

Joe is shivering at the side of the bath and I quickly wrap him in the towel.

'Your turn, Poppie.'

I lift her in and start to soap her, but when I bathe her private parts she cringes.

'Does it hurt down there, baby?'

'It's not Kobus,' she says quickly.

'It's alright, sweetheart.' I turn to Joe. 'Do you want to tell me anything?'

He looks like he's ready to talk but then decides it's time to go and watch TV.

When I'm towelling Poppie dry, we sing some nursery rhymes until Poppie stops in the middle of a line.

'Why won't Kobus leave me alone, Breda?'

I don't know what to say.

'Even Momma has asked him not to kick me while I'm feeling tired.'

He shouldn't kick you at any time. 'I know, sweetheart. Listen, you try and rest.'

'Where is he now, Breda?'

'Just gone to the store. Come and lie down and we'll watch some TV with Joey.' I bring her little blanket for her to lie on.

'My stomach hurts.'

'I know, baby. Shh, here comes Mommy.'

'What's the matter with her now?'

'She's tired, Auntie Lou. Can we let her rest?'

'She wet the bed again last night.'

'I'll clean it all up, Auntie. You don't need to do anything.'

'Kobus is going crazy with these dirty kids.'

'They can't help it. It's because he scares them so much.'

'Maybe.' Aunt Louisa sighs, and for a moment, I feel like I'm seeing the real Louisa. 'He scares me too sometimes.'

'Then you can understand how it is for the kids, Auntie.'

Her face has turned to stone again. 'But they keep messing everywhere, then I get it from Kobus. It's time they learnt how to be clean. Then we wouldn't have all this trouble.'

'Auntie, Poppie's privates are sore and swollen.'

'Don't be stupid. If you can't manage the simple task of bathing them without making a fuss, I'd better do it from now on.'

'No, Auntie, I didn't mean …'

'Kobus and I will bathe the kids. Got it? Don't you do it again.'

I want to say more, but I've tried before, and she always blames the kids. I stroke Poppie's hair. When did it get so thin? When did *she* get so thin? Seeing them every day, I guess I hadn't noticed, but looking down at her now, I see how pale and skinny she is.

'Glad I've caught you, Breda.

I'm collecting Poppie from daycare. 'Yes, Mrs Schuman?'

'What's happened to Poppie's head?'

I feel so stupid. My little cousins have so many bruises, I'd hardly noticed the big one on her face. 'I'm not sure, Mrs Schuman. Poppie, what happened?'

'It got hurt.'

'I know, sweetheart. But how did it get hurt?'

I'm sure I hear her whisper, 'Ko' but then she goes on to say that she fell.

The teacher gives me a meaningful look. 'And how come her head's been shaved?'

Again, I'm embarrassed. I'd watched her parents grab hold of her and shave her head just for the hell of it, but I'd done nothing to help her. 'I think she had lice,' I say, red-faced.

Mrs Schuman folds her arms and sighs. 'It's not right, Breda. And I think you know it.'

'Will you tell someone? Please.'

She nods, patting Poppie's head. 'I will. And I know you look out for them, Breda. But I think they need more than that now.'

I nod and sigh. I do my best. What more can I do?

'Hey, kids!' It's Jaco, our next door neighbour. 'You want to come over and play with Rudolf?'

Poppie is bouncing with excitement.

'It's cold out there, kids,' I say. But I can't resist Poppie's big blue eyes. 'Okay. Sure, Jaco. Thanks.' I look at Kobus; I should have asked him first. But he nods.

Jaco's dog is as gentle as a lamb with the kids.

'You're getting skinny, Poppie,' says Jaco. 'You could practically ride on Rudy's back!'

Poppie looks ready to clamber up.

'Hold on, girlie!' laughs Jaco. 'I was just kidding!'

Poppie hugs the dog instead. 'I love him,' she says quietly.

'And he loves you, baby,' says Jaco.

Joe's shivering. The kids don't have winter coats.

'Why don't you kids run around the yard with Rudolf? Keep you warm.'

Poppie and Joe scoot off.

I glimpse Kobus watching from the doorway. He's scowling; he hates to see the kids having fun. I watch him slowly pick up the garden hose and make a half-hearted attempt to spray the yard. Suddenly, he turns the hose on Poppie and Joe, drenching them to the skin as they stand there in shock.

'What the hell are you doing, Kobus?' yells Jaco, as his dog yelps and runs for shelter under the truck. 'Come here, kids. I'll get you a towel.'

'Don't move a muscle,' orders Kobus.

'But it's freezing, Uncle Kobus,' I say.

He briefly flicks the hose towards me, but only wets my shoes, before turning it on my little cousins again, roaring at them that they're filthy pigs.

My aunt appears at last. But before I can appeal to her for help, she's screaming. 'You just want to fuck each other!'

It feels like a bad dream. My aunt shouting obscenities at her three- and five-year-old kids, while her husband continues to soak them with the icy water. Jaco has grabbed a blanket from his seat on the walkway and is moving towards the children.

'Inside, you two,' roars my uncle, and they run to the house, with Aunt Louisa still yelling about them fucking each other.

'You, wait outside,' says Kobus, and he slams the door in my face.

I'm sobbing as Jaco grabs me in a hug.

'What the hell's going on, Breda?'

'I don't know! I mean, he beats them a lot, but … I don't understand this!'

'I'll call the police,' says Jaco.

'I wish they'd come out here and see what's happening. But they never do.'

'I'm going to try them again, Breda. Will you back me up?'

'Of course! But why did my auntie say those things? There's something weird going on, Jaco.'

'Is that animal hurting her, you know, down there too, Breda?'

'I think he must be. They all sleep in the same bed sometimes. Oh God, this needs to stop.'

'I'll get onto the cops. We'll make them listen.'

Over the next few days, I wait for the police to arrive. They don't come.

'Shh.' I put my finger to my lips. Joe does the same. Then Poppie follows suit. I've made it into a game for them, so that neither of them are as scared as I am.

I can tell Joe feels important as he carries his little bag and leads Poppie by the hand. She stumbles a little, and holds onto her stomach, but she can still walk, thank goodness.

The screen door is locked and the key isn't in its usual place.

'Wait here, kids,' I whisper, frantically wondering where on earth it can be.

Joe and Poppie sit down at the kitchen table, Joe putting his finger to his lips to remind Poppie to stay quiet.

One of the drawers. It's got to be in one of the kitchen drawers. Oh, why did I decide on tonight? We could have escaped quite easily when they were both at work in the café. But after the kicking Kobus gave Poppie this evening, I just can't let them suffer anymore. Finally, in the last drawer, I find it.

'Got it, kids,' I whisper. Poppie's head is lolling, and once we're out in the yard I take her in my arms, as Joe and I run as fast as we can.

The outdoor light floods the yard and the street beyond. How could I have forgotten about it?

Think, Breda, think!

But it's too late, Kobus is at the door and shouting that he'll kill us all.

We all get a 'hiding', right there and then, and every night for a week. For once, it's me who gets the worst of it, and I'm glad. It was my stupid fault and I've made the kids suffer even more. I should've planned it better. I'll try again though. When they least expect it.

After the week of beatings is over, Kobus is back to just the regular kicking and yelling and half drowning the kids.

When Aunt Louisa gives me a day off, I don't want to leave the kids alone with their parents. But I really need a break, so I go for a sleepover at my friend Alice's. We giggle and talk about boys, put makeup on each other, and swear to be friends forever. It's good to feel like a normal teenager for a while.

As I walk through the town on my way home the following day, I notice that the café is shut, with a sign on the door saying they've gone away. I quicken my pace towards the house. The truck isn't on the driveway and the door is locked. The spare key is still under the flowerpot.

I wander through each room, looking for signs of life. The stove is cold. The beds have been stripped, revealing their ugly stains of blood, urine and faeces. I open every cupboard and drawer. All the halfway decent stuff is gone, but among the bits of rubbish I spot a tiny slip of paper. It's a message in Joe's handwriting: '*We gon. Love yu Bre. Joe Pop xx*'. I stop myself from falling to the filthy floor. They've gone. But where to? They got me out of the way, so they could leave without telling me anything.

I'm startled by a knock on the outer door. It's our neighbour.

'Jaco! Where've they gone?'

He shakes his head. 'I don't know, Breda. Looks like they did a flit in the middle of the night.'

'The kids, Jaco! What's going to happen to the kids without anyone to watch out for them?'

He holds out his arms. 'I don't know, hon. I'll get on to the police again, but …'

All the fear I've been feeling for Poppie and Joe comes rising through my body as this kindly man I know so little about holds me tenderly.

'Where are you going to go, Breda?'

'My sister. I can go to my sister's place.'

'Give me your number. If I can find anything out, I'll let you know. The kids' school and daycare must know something.'

My sister and me fought like ferrets in a bag when we were younger, but now we're the best of friends, in spite of the age difference. She and her husband are trying for kids, with no luck yet, but she still loves to go shopping in Mother's World, and I enjoy mooching up and down the aisles with her, thinking of what I'd like to buy for Poppie and Joe. If only I knew where they were, I'd send them these cute sailor suits that are on sale today.

'Still no news of where that bitch took them?' My sister, who can read my mind, never had any time for Aunt Louisa.

'Not a peep out of them, or out of anyone else who might know.'

'Try not to worry, Bre. Hey, come on, let's go grab a coffee. My feet are killing me. And I've got something to tell you.'

She squeezes into the booth with our cappuccinos.

'You sure you're not pregnant?' I tease her. 'If you're not, someone needs to go on a diet!'

'Actually, I *am* pregnant, sis.'

'What? How come you didn't say anything? That's fantastic!'

'That's what I wanted to tell you. Yeah, yeah it's great.'

'You don't look like it's great, sis. Is everything okay?'

She passes me the Herald.

On the cover is a familiar face. At first I can't take it in. What I'm looking at can't be real.

My sister reaches across the table and takes my hand.

I look from the paper to her ashen face and back again. 'Poppie! Oh no, not Poppie! Please tell me that's not Poppie.'

But it's Poppie alright. I was there when that photo was taken. She's wearing her favourite pink dress, her blonde hair gathered into bunches. I kiss her picture. 'Poppie, oh Poppie, sweetheart. What did they do to you?'

* I rarely use the names of siblings and other children in my stories, and may use fictional characters, such as Breda, who is based on a number of people in Poppie's life.

An Overview of Poppie's Case

Poppie Van der Merwe
aged 3 years and 2 months
09.08.13 - 25.10.16
Brits, South Africa

The beauty of the South African plains, teeming with wildlife, and bordered by the Atlantic and Indian Oceans, belies a country fraught with centuries of injustice and apartheid. Political violence may have decreased since the freeing of ANC leader, Nelson Mandela, after 27 years' incarceration, but it has not gone away, and violence in all forms remains a reminder of the country's turbulent past and its enduring inequalities.

And in places where there is a culture of male sexual entitlement, women and girls are still seen by some as 2nd class citizens, with the incidence of rape at high levels, and the likelihood of long sentences for this crime almost non-existent. Could this mindset have allowed a little girl to be brutalised, sexually tortured and abused to death? Or is it yet another example of the worldwide atrocity that allows children to be treated as targets for the built-up rage of inadequate adults?

When Poppie was born, on 9 August 2013 (by coincidence, I'm writing this on that very date, nine years later), she was given the same name as her mother; Louisa Cornelia Susanna. But with her bright blue eyes and porcelain skin, it is easy to see why the new arrival was always known as Poppie, a word that means doll in Afrikaans. Tragically, in the months before she died, she was treated as no more than a plaything by her 'caregivers'.

Poppie's mother, Louisa, was born in 1974, in a small town in the Eastern Cape, South Africa. Like so many of the murderers I write about, Louisa's was a grim childhood. Her father died when she was ten years old, and she later reported that her new stepfather abused her; physically, emotionally and sexually.

Louisa soon moved away from her home town and married Freddie Els, but after their two children were born, the couple divorced.

Louisa then began a relationship with Johan Van Der Merwe, known as Christo, a diesel mechanic, and Louisa's third child, a son was born, followed by Poppie's arrival two years later. When Christo lost his job, he began drinking, and the relationship with his wife broke down, with Louisa taking out a protection order for herself and the kids. Poppie only saw her father a handful of times afterwards, although they spoke on the phone every fortnight.

Meanwhile, Louisa took her family to live with her mum, Susan, in the Southern Cape.

Orania is a town where only white people can live and work, with a view to the preservation of Afrikaner culture. People who want to live in Orania must undergo a vetting procedure, demonstrating fidelity to Afrikaans language and heritage, a commitment to employing only white Afrikaners, and adhering to various conservative Christian practices. Unmarried couples, for instance, cannot live together. The town even has its own currency.

The move proved to be a fateful one for Louisa and her children.

Louisa found work as a cashier in an OK store, where she met her next husband, Kobus Koekemoer.

Koekemoer had grown up in Pretoria, and once again, was badly treated by his stepfather. He was a bright student, and attended university, gaining a diploma which would have allowed him to work as a qualified electrician. Instead, the young Kobus joined the army to train as a chef. Prior to meeting Louisa, he had two children from previous relationships, but I believe that he had little contact with them.

In September 2015, Louisa and her children moved into Kobus Koekemoer's flat. As both adults were working, at around the age of 14, Louisa's elder daughter acted more as a mother than a sister to her young siblings, making sure the little ones were fed, clothed and loved. Poppie called her big sister 'Ma' or 'Mum'. The older girl remembers pulling little Poppie around in a box, in a game they called 'train-train'.

Two months after Louisa and her children moved in, Koekemoer and Louisa were married. The following day, they asked the oldest girl, who was so loved by her younger siblings, to move out. Rumour has it that Koekemoer literally pushed her out of the house, and she moved back in with her dad, Freddie, who lived in Despatch, a town in the Eastern Cape, far away from her siblings.

It is said that Koekemoer ran the house with an iron fist. He began giving the children harsh discipline with 'hidings' (beatings), often, allegedly, at Louisa's request. Discipline took the form of kicking, hitting, biting and throwing the two kids against the walls. They were also denied food. All four occupants shared the same bed, and Louisa and Kobus would have sex with the children present.

Soon, Jaco Roux, who became known to the children as Uncle Jaco, moved in next door, and although the two homes were so close together that they shared a walkway, he didn't notice anything odd at first. The children adored Jaco's puppy, Rudolf, and loved to play with him, and chatter to their neighbour. But in time, Jaco noticed that the two kids were solemn when their parents were around. In fact, he described that in their parents' presence, they became like 'tin soldiers'. And bit by bit, he saw less of the children outside the property.

One winter's day, when Jaco was talking to his neighbour, Koekemoer suddenly turned on the children, spraying them with the garden hose. Made to remain seated, soaking wet and freezing, to Jaco's alarm, Louisa then came out and yelled at the children that they had 'wanted to fuck each other'. One can scarcely imagine a household in which a mother shouts this at her three- and five-year-old children. At the very least, it certainly implies a warped attitude to sex, and with bruising found to Poppie's vagina after her death, their stepfather was accused of sexual abuse along with various other elements of cruelty and torture.

By the time Koekemoer and Jaco had become less neighbourly, due to alleged scratches to a motorbike, Jaco could hear Poppie screaming night and day, and he had begun reporting the Koekemoers for inappropriate discipline.

Jaco later testified that one August evening, he heard Kobus shouting at Poppie, "You just climbed in to cack in the bed". I feel that much can be inferred by such shaming statements uttered to a young girl living in fear; the lack of care and respect is plain to see.

The neighbour also said that when he once asked Kobus why Poppie had a plaster cast on her leg, Koekemoer went crazy with anger, and Louisa said that Poppie had fallen down the stairs.

Jaco reported several incidents, but didn't see any response; in four months, the police did nothing based on these reports. Jaco felt they didn't take them seriously and wouldn't get involved in domestic disputes. The neighbour saw a slight response from child protection agencies, and a social worker would occasionally be sent out in response to Jaco's reports.

During their time in Orania, Kobus and Louisa ran a café in the town, and the children attended school and daycare.

Tanya Goosen was a teacher at an aftercare centre, who told the court that Poppie's brother, who had previously been calm and good natured, suddenly began to have angry outbursts (such as rolling around on the ground, screaming and hitting other children). Louisa and Kobus suggested spraying the five-year-old with cold water. Ms Goosen took photos of the little boy's bruising, and he slowly revealed a little of how they'd come about, including the use of a long wooden porridge spoon and kicking in the stomach.

Before too long, he was showing up in girls' clothing, and shoes that were much too big for him, and even wearing a heavy winter coat in summer that he refused to take off, for fear of angering his mother and stepfather.

When his parents came to pick him up from school, the terrified child would run and hide in the bathroom.

Poppie's daycare teacher, Esna Schuman, took a photo of Poppie with a huge bruise on her forehead that Louisa explained away by saying that her daughter had bumped her head against the car. But Poppie disclosed that Louisa had punched her with a closed fist. Ms Schuman also reported that Poppie had her head shaved right down to her scalp, as one might do as part of the treatment for lice, which Poppie did not have.

Louisa Koekemoer later admitted that she had hidden Poppie's injuries from Heidi Smit, the school counsellor.

Another observer of the children was Dr Becker, who was shocked at the changes in the little girl over just a few short months. On examination, he found that Poppie had multiple bruises, and stiffened in apparent terror as the doctor approached her.

On 5 August 2016, the doctor found bruises and cuts on Poppie's ears, and reported these injuries on the child's hospital file, but there is no evidence that he also reported to child protection services. (My apologies if this was in fact done.)

By September 2016, with the outward signs of injury becoming increasingly visible to observers, the Koekemoers shut down their café, and made their escape during the night. Their destination was an isolated smallholding at Mamogaleskraal, near Brits, in Pretoria. Now, with neither child enrolled in school or daycare, there was no one watching and the abuse was given free rein.

It is hard to imagine more horrific lives than the ones led by these beautiful children. Terrorised by their mother and stepfather, they were screamed at for soiling their beds and sundry 'misdemeanours'.

And now, there were no witnesses and no one to call for help.

On 25 October 2016, Kobus and Louisa arrived at Brits Provincial Hospital with Poppie in their arms. A paramedic's attempts to resuscitate the three-year-old were doomed to failure, as rigor was already setting in, and it wasn't possible to sufficiently open her jaw. It was almost certain that Poppie had been dead for a long time. When asked what had happened, her brother responded that Poppie would not eat.

Dr Roddy Gumbu examined the three-year-old, and pronounced her dead. Koekemoer told the doctor he'd been whipping Poppie when she collapsed. Take a breath with me, reader, as it seems he thought that whipping a defenceless child was reasonable behaviour. With bruising and swelling all over her body including her vagina, and a haematoma on her shaven head, on which there were several razor cuts, the doctor was ready to call the police.

Overhearing this, Koekemoer became furious and changed his story, saying his stepdaughter had been watching TV, had complained of feeling tired and then collapsed. He claimed to have tried to revive her by taking her into the bathroom and pouring water over her. Whilst Louisa cried and said little, Kobus further claimed that the bruising was caused by Poppie rolling around in the truck on the journey to the hospital.

Kobus Koekemoer was arrested that same evening. 45-year-old Louisa was not arrested until two months later. She was denied bail, as her life was in danger from the public, and she was also a suicide risk.

Poppie's autopsy revealed that the lower left area of her skull had filled with blood, and that blunt force trauma leading to catastrophic brain injury was the cause of death. The lump on her head was about the size of a tennis ball, and there were many old and new bruises on her body from being violently kicked.

During his initial court hearing, Kobus said "Poppie is with God now, where nobody can harm her. We do not know his plan for us." Once in custody, both the accused changed their tune, and soon each one was blaming the other.

Prior to her arrest on 2 November 2016, Louisa told a bizarre story about being kidnapped and assaulted by a blonde woman who ordered her to accompany her to Pretoria for questioning, but instead drove around for hours in a storm, claiming to be lost. The woman allegedly interrogated Louisa, saying she had to start telling the truth. She then stopped the car and beat Louisa on the face and head with gun-like object, which was later assumed to be a pellet gun. Louisa allegedly escaped to the safety of a gas station.

Louisa's version of the family set-up was that "Kobus often kicked Poppie in the stomach", denying that she had ever assaulted her child.

Although she had been present when her husband tortured her children, she had claimed, at the time, that they had fallen or accidentally bumped their heads.

On the fateful day, with Kobus out at the supermarket, she said that the house was peaceful, with her youngest child lying on a small mattress in front of the TV, drifting in and out of sleep. When her husband returned, he was in a foul mood, and ordered his wife to bring in the shopping, whilst demanding a drink.

On completing these chores, Louisa stated that Poppie was no longer in front of TV and that Kobus said: "She's playing dead in the bathroom again". Checking on her daughter, Louisa claimed that she was alarmed to see that Poppie was very still, with blue lips, and after attempts to resuscitate her failed, the family set off for the hospital.

Louisa added that she was terrified of Koekemoer, saying that he was extremely strict and domineering, and used physical abuse against the children regularly, and that he had threatened to kill her several times.

She then immediately said "We were such a close, happy family unit".

We are learning more and more about coercive control, and as I research the subject and gain more understanding, I do see how insidious it can be, and how the victim can feel compelled to behave in ways that are alien to most of us. Although it seems almost impossible to believe, this coercion appears to lead some victims to abuse their own children, or at least to stand by and do little or nothing in the face of their torture. I cannot say if this was the case for Louisa Koekemoer. We need to learn much more about this possible facet of child abuse.

Interestingly, Louisa also said: "I never thought it would go that far." This is an admission that she knew wrongdoing was taking place, but that she didn't recognise the significance of kicking and throwing a small child around the room. It seems to genuinely take some murdering caregivers by surprise when such actions "go that far", ie result in death. They are nonplussed at the outcome of their so-called discipline.

This minimising of violence crops up time and again in abused to death cases.

Kobus later repeats this viewpoint at his trial, saying that he had given the little girl a serious hiding (beating) with a wooden spoon whenever she was naughty, but he denied having had anything to do with her death.

Wearing a tuxedo-style suit at his bail hearing, Koekemoer said he wanted to be able to go to his church in Brits, saying, "I want to forgive people, as God forgave my sins".

He offered a variety of explanations for Poppie's death, including her having had episodes where she suddenly stopped breathing, that she could've been injured the previous weekend when playing with her cousins, and that his wife had said there was a history of epilepsy, asthma and heart disease in her family.

He added that the three-year-old was not a little angel, that she was very rough, to the extent of bullying her older brother. Is he blaming Poppie for her own death?

Bail was denied.

Kobus' story of the day Poppie was murdered revolved around the actions of his wife. In a bad temper due to Poppie having had an accident while being potty trained, Louisa allegedly made Poppie eat her breakfast in her bedroom, saying, "I don't want to see you".

Both Poppie and the bed were soaking, and Louisa's fury escalated as she screamed and threw her daughter across the room. When Poppie hit her head against the wall, she became dazed and walked into the wall again, and then fell down. Louisa then dragged Poppie by the arm and put her into the bath to hose her down; a common practice in that household.

Kobus went out to the mall, and on his return, Poppie was lying by the trash bin. He called out to his wife, "Poppie's playing dead again".

They both left her lying there alone for two or three hours, and when Kobus went to check on her, Poppie hadn't moved; she was cold and her lips were blue.

Kobus and Louisa Koekemoer both pleaded not guilty to the charges of murder, and assault with intent to cause GBH. They were found guilty, however, and sentenced on 24 May 2018 by Judge Bert Bam at Goateng in the Pretoria High Court.

At the sentencing hearing, Louisa claimed again that she was terrified of Kobus, saying that he had threatened to kill her and the children if she tried to get help for them. She admitted that she had never stopped her husband from hurting the children.

A prison pastor told the court that Louisa had now become a "child of God" and Louisa stated that she served as "an example for my children as I learnt from my mistakes".

Nevertheless, along with her husband, she was sentenced to life in prison, which in South Africa is 25 years, and they were both also sentenced to an extra ten years for child abuse to Poppie and a five-year-old boy.

Poppie's birth father, Christo Van der Merwe, was not allowed access to his former partner and their children. But listening to the recording he made of his last phone conversation with his little girl, or reading the transcript which follows, you can decide for yourself about the level of affection in their relationship. Poppie tells her daddy that she is watching television, and endearingly, that she is still small. She then sings the popular Afrikaner children's folk song, 'Hansie Slim' for him. I understand that Mr Van der Merwe recorded all such phone conversations with his children. I can only conclude that they were precious to him.

Here's the link for one such phone call, if you'd like to listen to it: **https://bit.ly/3dTdyxl**

Hearing Poppie's voice reminds me how very young she was. And do you think Christo is calling her 'My chicken' or is that my imagination?

Below is a rough transcript of some of their last conversations. I apologise if there is any confusion, as it jumps about a little. The part-conversation from the above link begins at the point when someone coughs on the tape.

Poppie: Hello, Daddy

Christo: Hello, my little girl. What are you doing?

Poppie: I'm watching TV

Christo: Watching TV? That's lovely my little girl. What else can you tell Daddy?

Poppie: Daddy

Christo: Yes, my little girl?

Poppie: I'm watching TV, Daddy

Christo: Oh, are you watching TV?

Poppie: Yes

Christo: And are you growing up very nicely?

Poppie: Yes, I'm the smallest

(Someone coughs in the background)

Poppie: Daddy, I'm small

Christo: Are you small?

Poppie: The smallest small, yes

Christo: Oh, mmm

Poppie: Daddy, I want to sing Hansie Slim

Christo: Sing Hansie Slim for me

Poppie: Hansie Slim, berg wil klim, stok en hoed, pas hom goed (English translation: Clever (or little) Hansel, wants to climb mountains, a stick and hat suit him well.)

Christo: Yes

Poppie: Daddy, I want to sing (inaudible)

Christo: Okay

It is comforting to know that Poppie was loved by her siblings and other family members.

My thanks to my reader Caroline C, from South Africa, for alerting me to Poppie's story

Rest Safely in Peace, Poppie

Prevention of Poppie's Death

If only one of several courses of action had been taken, Poppie could have been saved.

1 – If only one of the two adults living in the home had put a stop to the abuse.

It may sound simplistic, but if just one of the adults had changed the patterns being played out, family life would have been very different. It's possible that Louisa was a victim of Kobus, and under his coercive control, making it extremely difficult to break away, even if she loved her children.

Although controlling men (or women) can be very adept at isolating their partners, if she had confided in family or friends, she could have got the support she needed.

Her mother, with whom Louisa lived when she first moved to Orania, and who was present at her daughter's trial, appears to have given support, although we don't know to what extent. Running a café, Louisa must have had many acquaintances, and possibly some friends, that she could perhaps have confided in.

I cannot trace a women's refuge in Orania, although they do exist in the Northern Cape.

2 – If only medical staff had reported more effectively.

Making notes in a medical report is extremely helpful in plotting patterns of events and injuries to children. However, if serious concerns, as there was in Poppie's case, are not reported to child protection services, these events can fly under the radar. It could have made the world of difference if everyone involved had record, reported and worked together. Which leads to my next point ...

3 – If only those reporting the abuse had been taken more seriously.

We know that the Koekemoer's neighbour, Jaco, reported several times, and that teachers did the same. I assume the teachers realised that Poppie's brother was not merely 'acting up' when he began to be violent towards his classmates, he was reaching out. If these reports had been appropriately followed up by child protection services, and then by the police, care proceedings could have been initiated that could have made the difference between life and death.

4 – If only the family had been checked upon when they disappeared after the abuse had been revealed.

The family fled the area but the authorities did not trace the children in order to monitor them, despite their suspiciously hasty departure. Poppie and her brother had been attending school and pre-school, so did their parents claim they were now being homeschooled? Homeschooling by abusive parents should not be allowed. Period.

5 – If only the adults had been educated about toileting.

Much of the cruelty originated in fury at the children's toilet accidents. It is tragic that a basic bodily function, that a young child is just learning how to control, is used as a weapon against them, and soon becomes a cyclical nightmare, as terrifying a child, or indeed an adult, is pretty much a guarantee that they will soil themselves. This ignorance and intolerance needs to end, as it is one of the primary triggers for violence in caregivers of young children.

6 – If only Louisa had been more wary of bringing a new stepfather into the family.

The most prolific perpetrators of child abuse in all its forms (including sexual, neglect, etc) are stepparents, often, though by no means exclusively, male. For the sake of the children a parent needs to take time to find out as much as they can about the person who will have access to their babies.

7 – If only Louisa (and possibly Kobus) had been able to break the cycle of abuse.

This is the big one. If they had resisted the impulse to repeat the abuse they had experienced in their own childhood, Poppie would not have suffered so much and could have lived. There are support groups for parents who feel they are at risk of continuing the cycle of generational abuse, and I feel that this is one of the ways forward. I am going to investigate this much further, as this is the key to prevention.

We know from many examples, including those from my own readers who have confided in me, that the cycle *can* be broken.

If You Tell – Buried Alive

I'm teaching my friend Izabel some new skipping tricks, but she keeps tripping over the rope.

'Oh, Iz!'

She laughs. 'I think I need to practice!'

'Just a bit.'

'It's cos the boys are watching us. I can't concentrate.'

I glance over at my brother and his friends kicking a football around. 'Them? Just ignore them.'

'I wonder if they like us, Gabi?'

I snort. 'What? We're only nine, Izzy!'

'I know, but … Anyway, I'm nearly ten!'

'Boys are just silly. Kicking a ball around like that. They all think they're Pelé.'

'Nothing wrong with that,' she laughs. 'He *is* our most famous celebrity.'

'Yeah, and he's ancient. Older than my grandma.'

Izabel tries again with the skipping rope, and falls against me.

'Come on,' I say. 'Let's go for a soda.'

We sit near the open window, shaded by the canopy.

'Can I ask you something, Gabi?'

'Yeah, course, Iz.'

'You never seem to talk about boys like I do with my other friends.'

'Oh,' I say. 'What do you talk about?'

'Just stuff. Like maybe kissing a boy some day.'

'Oh gross! Are you kidding me? I don't like any boy like that. I'm just a kid, Izabel, and you're not much older.'

'I guess five months makes a difference.'

I shrug. 'Maybe.'

'But I like Javier, Gab,' says Izabel. 'I wouldn't mind if he tried to kiss me.'

Javier's my brother's best friend. 'Eeuww, that's disgusting!' I say. 'So that's why you wanted to stay and watch the game.'

'Yeah,' she nods. 'But I think it's you he likes, Gabi.'

'Oh yuk! I wish you hadn't said that, Izzy.'

'I don't know for sure.'

'Look, I wouldn't bother with him, if I was you, Iz.'

'Don't say that. He's gorgeous.'

All this boy talk has grossed me out. 'Want to go window shopping? I think there's new unicorn charms at the store.'

'Where're you going, Mom?'

She's looking very pleased with herself. 'You think I look nice?'

I nod. Even my brother nods.

'Good. Your mom's made a new friend.'

'Boy or girl?' I ask.

My brother pushes me. 'She wouldn't be so dressed up for a girl, you idiot!'

'Oh, okay.'

'He's a great guy, kids. So if I bring him back home, behave yourselves.'

'We will, Mom. But you won't bring him back, will you? I thought we were going to watch TV together.'

She tosses her head. She has long brown hair like mine. Sometimes people think she's my big sister. 'Don't try and tell me what to do, Gabi. I've told you about that.'

'Sorry, Mom. Your hair looks nice.'

Mom's a hairdresser. Her hair always looks nice. She touches up her lipstick.

'See you later. Behave yourselves.'

'Okay. Have a great time.'

My brother's three years older than me, so it's okay to leave us at home without a baby-sitter, though Mom doesn't go out very often. I'm hoping he'll make pancakes later, and he might let me play on his X-box. But he's straight onto his phone, texting.

'Javier and Luis are coming over.'

'Oh no. I thought it was just gonna be us.'

'Sorry, little sis. Hanging out with the guys tonight.'

'But you're staying home?'

''Course I am.'

I go into the kitchen and make myself a sandwich and grab a soda. 'I'll leave you to it then. I'll be up in my room.'

'Okay, kid. Have fun.'

I hear them arrive and Javier asking where I am. I push the chest up against the door.

He knocks. 'Gabi? Gabi, is it okay to say Hi?'

'Hi,' I say. 'I'm busy, Jav. Doing my homework.'

'See you at school then?

'Yeah. Will do.'

He goes back downstairs. That was easy, thank goodness. But I wonder if Mom would let me put a lock on my bedroom door?

I flop onto my bed and flick through one of Mom's magazines. 'Who's the ideal man for you?' 'How to keep your man happy.' '10 things you didn't know he liked.' *Who cares about all that?*

Mom likes her new boyfriend very much. His name is André, and he's a lot older than Mom. She doesn't get so mad at us as she did before, so we're happy about that!

'Gabi is so pretty, Emileide. Were you so pretty when you were Gabi's age?'

'Of course,' says Mom. 'Even prettier. And people say now that we look like sisters.'

'Perhaps they need glasses!' laughs André.

I catch one of Mom's cold looks.

'And this one,' says André, turning to my brother. 'He's clever. Doing well at school, hey? You must be proud of them, Em. You're doing a good job with them.'

The cold look is replaced by a smile. 'If you say so, André!'

'I do. Now come here and give me a hug. All of you, come on, let's have a family hug.'

Being the smallest, I feel like I'm suffocating when the hug seems to go on forever.

'Right,' says Mom at last, and I can breathe again. 'Gabi, come and help me in the kitchen.'

'I don't want to see you in that skirt again!'

I look down at myself. 'But it's clean, Mom. I'm not disrespecting you.'

'Go upstairs and change. You look like a whore!'

'A what, Mom? I don't understand. You just bought it for me. Don't you remember? I thought you loved me in it.'

'Well, I've changed my mind. Go and put the blue one on. Go on.'

I come back down wearing the skirt she used to say made me look like a grandmother.

'That's better. And don't let me see you in any of those other ones again.'

'Which other ones, Mom?'

'The short ones, you imbecile.'

I don't mind what I wear as long as Mom is happy. 'Oh, okay.'

'Oh, okay,' she mimics me.

I stand in the doorway, not knowing what to do.

'Oh, get back to your room. I don't want to see you around when André gets here.'

I've finished my homework, so I tidy my room a bit, then talk to Izzy for a while. Suddenly, I hear loud voices from the living room.

'I saw you, you liar. I saw you!'

'Calm down, Em. I've done nothing wrong.'

'Oh, she's so pretty. Oh, how nice you look today, Gabi.'

What are they saying about me?

'Stop shouting! And don't try to tell me what to say or where to look.'

My brother turns up his music, so I can't hear much more. In between the tracks I can tell it's gone quiet again downstairs, so I change into my pj's, then pick up my book and read until I fall asleep.

I'm half awake when I sense something different in the room. I think I can hear breathing. I freeze. Someone is in here. I squeeze my eyelids shut, until I'm sure I hear a soft tread heading towards the door and then it closing gently behind them.

'Mom.'

She's reading the newspaper. 'Uh-huh?'

'There was someone in my bedroom last night. Did you come in?'

She frowns. 'No, and don't tell lies, Gabi.'

'But I'm not, I definitely heard someone.'

'Stop it. Stop being so silly.'

'Hey, Emi,' says André. 'Don't be too hard on her. It's not a bad thing to have a good imagination.'

'I don't want her telling lies.'

'Neither do I, but I don't want her being scared either. I'll see her safely into bed tonight.'

'No, it's alright,' I say quickly. 'I'm sure now; I just imagined it.'

'Maybe, sweetheart. But I'll check that you're okay, just in case.'

'No, really. You don't have to …'

André puts his finger to his lips. 'Quiet now, Gabi. I'll look after you.'

I'm reading 'Harry Potter and the Goblet of Fire' for the umpteenth time when I hear the faint knocking.

'It's just me, sweetheart.'

He pushes open the door. 'Ahh, you look safe and well, Gabi. In fact, you look better than well. You look beautiful; all cosied up in bed.'

'Yes, I'm fine tonight, André. I definitely think I imagined it last night.'

'Maybe, maybe not.' He comes nearer to my bed. 'But who could blame anyone for coming into your room? Even just to watch you sleep.'

I try to laugh. 'Wouldn't *that* be weird!'

'Not really, honey. I know lots of Dads who want to watch over their kids. Keep them safe from bad men.'

'Oh.'

'Move your legs over a bit, sweetheart.' He sits down on the bed, and strokes the hair back off my forehead. 'You really are a very pretty young lady, Gabi.'

What do I say? What do I say? 'Oh, thank you.'

He pats my leg through the sheet. 'Sleep well, beautiful. There's nothing to worry about now I'm here.'

I hear the soft footstep on the landing outside my room. Maybe he won't come in tonight. Maybe everything will go back to how it was. But the handle slowly turns.

'Just checking you're okay, my beautiful girl.' He sits down on the bed. 'Hey, you're all wrapped up like a burrito.'

I need to stop doing that, because I think he enjoys unwrapping me. But at least I feel safer for those first few minutes.

'I can't stay long tonight, my sweetheart.'

'Please don't hurt me again, Papa André.'

'I won't, my angel. I won't. Aren't I always very gentle?'

Asking him to stop never works, so I try something different. 'I'll tell Mom.'

He grabs both of my wrists. 'If you tell, your Mom will be very upset with you. She might send you away.'

And I know he's right.

'So you won't tell, will you?'

'No. No, I won't.'

'That's a good girl.'

When he finishes, he looks me straight in the eye and reminds me, 'If you tell …'

And I don't tell. I don't tell for a long, long time.

Mom is grinning like the Cheshire Cat. 'André is going to be your new Papa.'

'How come?' says my brother. 'We already have our Papa.'

'We're going to get married. So André will be your stepfather. Okay?'

'Well, yes. It's okay, I guess.'

'It's great, isn't it, Gabi?'

'Yes, yes it's great.'

'Girl, you're so grumpy these days. What's got into you? Aren't you happy for your mom?'

'I–I don't know.'

She grabs my upper arms and squeezes. 'Well, cheer yourself up or I'm going to be really mad at you. You know what I mean?'

'Yes, Mom.'

André comes into the kitchen. 'You tell them, Em?'

'Yeah, just now. They're so excited for us.'

André holds out his arms. 'This calls for a family hug.'

And I have to join in, and André touches me where he shouldn't, right in front of Mom.

Izzy and me are sipping milkshakes in the park. We're still friends, even though she's gone up to high school now and I don't see quite as much of her.

'You're quiet these days, Gabi.'

'Am I?'

She gives me one of her looks. 'You know you are. What's bothering you? And what's with these long sleeves? It's roasting hot today.' She grabs one of the cuffs and pulls it up. 'Gabi! What's that?'

'Oh, it's nothing.'

'It doesn't look like nothing to me. That's a massive bruise!'

'Oh, you know what my brother's like when we start play-fighting.'

'Gabi, please tell me the truth. Someone is hurting you.'

I try to gulp down my tears, then take a deep breath. 'Mommy has started to beat me.'

She rolls my sleeve up even higher. 'That's a real beating, Gab.'

'Yeah, I know. I'm scared of her, Izzy.'

'Really? Your cute Mom?'

I nod. 'There's something else too.'

She puts her arm around my shoulder. That makes me cry. 'Go on, Gab.'

'It's Papa André.'

'What about him?'

'You know.'

'No, I don't know. Tell me.'

'He gets me on my own, and does things.' I let the silence hang between us until her puzzled look disappears.

'What! You mean he hurts you? Touches you in your private places?'

I can only nod.

'Oh, hon. What does your mom say?'

'I tried to tell her once, but she didn't really listen. She looked pretty mad at me for trying. It was after that she started beating me.'

'You need to make her listen, Gab. When she really knows she'll take care of it.'

'I'll try. I just want it to stop. I'm scared all the time. Even when he just looks at me. I feel dirty, and it hurts so much.'

'How long has it been happening, Gab?'

'Since Mom met him.'

'Gabi, that's nearly two years!' She holds me closer and tells me everything is going to be alright.

On Saturday morning, my brother is outside playing football as usual, and my stepfather is sleeping. I'm going to tell her. I'll tell her about him coming into my room at night. And then she'll understand why I don't always feel like smiling, and why I beg her not to go out and leave me alone with him.

'Mom.'

'Uh-huh.' She's watching TV.

'Mom, I want to tell you something and don't be mad.'

'Can't it wait, Gabi? You can see I'm watching my programme.'

'I know, Mom. I'm sorry.' I know if I don't tell her now, I'll lose courage. 'Please, Mom. I have to tell you now.'

She slaps me. 'Just wait! Go and clean the dishes and tidy the kitchen till I'm ready.'

I run the hot water into the bowl. If my stepfather wakes up, I won't be able to tell her. I hear the theme tune, and go and stand in the doorway, trembling. 'Mom.'

She's driving like a lunatic, heading way out of town. My brother and I are rolling around in the back of the car, holding onto to the door handles.

'Slow down, Mom,' yells my brother.

But instead, she speeds up, muttering the same words she screamed at me when I told her. 'You're a liar. I'll kill you. Keep away from my husband. You don't deserve to live any longer.'

I decide to try and make her stop. 'Mom, please.'

But she reaches round and punches me, almost running us off the road.

We turn off by the dump, then rumble down a dirt trail and shudder to a halt.

'Out. Both of you. Out.' She pushes me ahead of her as I stumble on the uneven ground. 'Keep walking, bitch.'

'Mom, you're scaring me.'

'Keep walking.'

I'm crying so hard, I can hardly see where I'm going.

'Stop. Right here.' Then she whirls me round and punches me in the face.

'Mom!' shouts my brother. 'Don't! Please don't.'

She takes hold of the electrical cable she's brought with her and waves it in my face. 'You don't deserve to live!'

I'm rooted to the spot, but my brother shouts, 'Run, Gabi,' and I follow him into the trees.

But I'm still dizzy from the punch, and I'm no match for Mom. She catches up to me easily and she grabs me, then loops the wire around my neck. And then she pulls.

'Mommy!' I try to scream.

My brother is watching from a short distance away. 'Mom! What are you doing? I thought you just meant to hit her!'

'Get over here now,' yells Mom. 'Or you'll get the same.'

She turns to me. 'I'll kill you, you little liar.' She punches my head and I fall to the ground. She kicks my stomach and I try to curl into a ball.

'Hold her down,' she yells to my brother.

'Mom! No!'

'Do it!'

He crouches beside me. 'I'm sorry, Gabi.'

'Do it!'

'I can't!'

I scream as Mom kicks my whole body, again and again. Blood is pouring from my head.

She's calling me nasty names the whole time, and trying to make my brother beat me. 'Put her in the hole.'

'What?'

'Put. Her. In. The. Hole.'

I feel my body being dragged and suddenly I can't breathe. I flail my arms and legs but I feel Mom stuffing me down, headfirst into the earth.

'Mom, what …' The rest of my brother's words are muffled as my ears, nose and mouth fill with dirt.

I kick my feet, trying to shout. 'Let me out. Help, let me out.' But after a short while, I faintly hear the car engine start up, and they drive away.

I try calling for help, as best I can, but more dirt just gets into my mouth. And I know this is an isolated place. People won't even come here to walk their dogs. It's up to me to save myself. I frantically try to push myself up towards the top of the hole, but every movement seems to jam me in tighter.

Am I going to die here?

Suddenly, I can make out a car approaching. It must be Mom. She's punished me enough and now she's come to dig me out.

Oh, thank you, Mom. I promise to be good and I won't say anything more about André, even if he carries on hurting me.

But all I feel is the thud of the dirt being packed even tighter around me, and the breath leaving my body for the last time.

An Overview of Gabi's Case

Gabrielly Magalhães de Souza
03.10.09 – 21.03.20
aged 10 years & 5 months
Brasilândia, Brazil

Gabrielly's mother, Emileide Magalhães, who was 29 years old at the time she murdered her daughter, was a hairdresser in Brasilândia. Perhaps, as an attractive young woman, she was accustomed to the admiration of those around her. After bearing three children, and marrying a handsome man 18 years her senior, she may have felt a little less secure in the power she had over men. This is simply my own speculation, as I try to understand what caused her to act as she did towards her daughter.

As an aside, it is my understanding that Emileide also abused both alcohol and cocaine.

Much of what we know about Gabi's final day is from the testimony of her 13-year-old brother.

Late in the morning of Saturday 21 March 2020, while her stepfather is asleep in another room, and her brother is outside playing, Gabi plucks up the courage to confide in her mother that her stepfather has been sexually abusing her. It has been going on for around two years. Instead of hearing her daughter out, comforting her and reassuring her that she will put an end to it, Emileide flies into a rage. When her brother comes indoors, he witnesses his mother yelling at Gabi, before turning to him and telling him what his sister has accused their stepfather of. Chillingly, Emileide says these words: "Gabi will not live any longer because the girl is a liar."

Emileide then picks up an electrical cable and the 13-year-old boy expects that she will beat Gabi with it; perhaps this was a regular practice in the home. Again, Emileide says ominously: "I'm going to end her life because I don't want my daughter to be talked about badly." In her fury, she not only focuses her anger on the victim rather than perpetrator, but she opts to blow the consequences for her daughter clear out of proportion by choosing death over any perceived shame. But perhaps it is because she knows it is not her daughter, but her beloved husband, and herself, who will be shamed.

Ordering the two children into the car, Emileide drives out of town, and turns off the street, onto a side road, near the town dump. Parking in a wooded area, she instructs the kids to get out of the car. Fearing what lies ahead, Gabi and her brother make a run for it, but Gabi is caught, and her mother puts electrical wire or cable around the ten-year-old's neck, and begins to strangle her.

Begging for her life, Gabi is beaten and knocked to the ground and (it is unclear how) lands head first in a hole. Her mother then begins to pack earth into the hole, burying the terrified child upside down. Emileide orders her son to help or risk getting the same treatment. After attempting to conceal Gabi's body, they jump into the car and drive back to town. Emileide then drops off her son in the Town Square, and goes for a beer.

It is hard to know what Emileide is thinking at this time. We can assume that, mulling it over, she must have wondered if she'd buried Gabi well enough, because she returns to the scene. Finding that her daughter is still alive, does she frantically claw at the earth with her bare hands in an effort to save Gabi's life? No, she does not. She may even pile more dirt into the hole to be certain that her daughter will not survive. Whatever the case, she drives off again, before returning a third and final time, to find that Gabi is dead.

That same evening, Emileide files a missing person's report, claiming that she had earlier dropped her two children off in the Town Square, but that Gabi has disappeared. A few hours later, however, she confesses to the crime. She claims that she went to the burial site alone.

Officers then interview Gabrielly's brother. Spotting lacerations on the boy's legs, indicating rough physical work, officers pump him for information. He eventually admits that he had been at the burial site, and that his mother had threatened him with a tire iron if he did not participate. Heart-breakingly, he reports that he had heard his sister crying out for help, and could see her feet moving as they stuck out of the grave.

During questioning by the police, and on the witness stand during Emileide's trial, Gabi's brother vouches for his sister, saying that he knew about André's abuse, and that he felt sure that his mother was also well aware of it.

However, Emileide sticks to her story that she did not know about the abuse, despite one of Gabi's friends saying that the girl had confided in her a year before her murder, and that Gabi had tried to tell her mother, but had been frightened by her reaction.

A strange part of Emileide's testimony (as if any part of this case is not strange), is that she says that Gabi fell into the hole by accident; that she didn't dig it nor put her in intentionally. Furthermore, she describes falling into hole herself along with Gabi then stepping on her child to lever herself up, causing Gabrielly to fall deeper inside. The judge naturally asks her why she didn't get her daughter out of the hole. She replies that she was out of her mind, and didn't know what she was doing.

The cause of Gabi's death was compressive asphyxia, but as her body was also covered in many bruises, it is suspected that she was also tortured. The Brazilian local media reported that the medical expert who examined Gabrielly's intimate parts said that they had become so injured and deformed that her vagina was comparable to that of a sexually active prostitute.

Gabi's stepfather, André Luiz Ferreira, was arrested for the sexual abuse, and was sentenced to 20 years for rape. He is incarcerated in Bataguassu Prison.

Her mother, Emileide Magalhães, is serving a 39 year sentence for her daughter's murder, in Três Lagoas Women's Prison.

Gabrielly's brother was initially hospitalised at Unei (Inpatient Educational Unit), a socio-educational detention centre, but was later released into the care of his birth father.

During the trial, in words reminiscent of other letters written to their torturers, such as Gabriel Fernandez, and Ayesha Ali, the prosecutor reads a letter in which Gabrielly apologises to her mother for being a terrible child, for not listening to her, and that from then on, she would obey her. She also writes:

> *I love you Mom. Thank you for existing. You're the most beautiful, smartest and the nicest mother in the entire world. I love you from the bottom of my heart.*

My grateful thanks to Luana, from the Facebook group, In Loving Memory of Little Gabrielly Magalhães de Souza, for alerting me to Gabi's story

Rest Safely in Peace, Gabrielly

Choosing a Partner over a Child

This is a phenomenon we see regularly in all cases of child abuse, not only those that end in murder. And according to my research, it is more often the woman than the man who elevates her partner above the safety and needs of her own children.

In days gone by, and, in some cultures, right up to the present day, women could not earn their own money, and were therefore financially dependent upon men. Tradition also dictated that a woman should be subservient to her husband, and so it's not difficult to see that without any power in the relationship, a woman might feel bound to subjugate herself, and her children, to the needs of the man.

However, for the most part, things are very different nowadays. Women can earn their own money, and even if they do not work, many countries have welfare systems that support those without an income.

Brazil's service appears to be a little complicated. There is a benefit system, but the sums paid are not very high, and the payment can be sporadic, with frequent delays. So I can imagine that this is still a consideration for single mothers.

But Emileide was a working mother, and it's unclear what support she would have needed or received. I'm just speculating, but it could have been a factor in holding on to a sexual predator at the expense of her daughter's life.

Apart from perceived financial advantages to being with a partner, social status is now more visible than it used to be, with social media everywhere we look, showing us having fun, spending money on meals and possessions, and being popular amongst friends and family. In the case of Emileide and André, there were hundreds of Facebook posts with the smiling couple looking out at the viewer, perhaps inciting a little envy of the well groomed, attractive pair. Several photos also showed a little girl, putting on a brave face despite her torture.

It is said that a huge number of children–7,000–are violently killed in Brazil each year.

A 2015 UNICEF report, *Progress and Challenges for Children and Adolescents in Brazil*, using figures from 2013, states that: "28 people under 19 were killed every day in Brazil".

Although the figure includes all types of violence, including gang, gun and drug crime, this death rate is higher than in war zones. Whichever way you look at it, this is a horrifically high number of children suffering and dying. Sadly, in addition to that, around 45,000 children are subjected to sexual violence. As in many, perhaps most, countries in the world, this shows that children's lives are seen as disposable.

Although a country with a growing economy, Brazil has significant issues of violence, corruption, crime and social inequality.

JESSICA JACKSON

Surveillance

The Family – 2019

'So, how was it, today?'

'The usual,' says Jennifer, bouncing the three-year-old on her knee. 'This one was an angel.'

'I know that,' says Al. 'What about the other one?'

'He messed himself again, Al.'

'He does it on purpose. You know that, right?'

'Sure do. And all that moving about. It's like he wants you to punish him, Al.'

He nods at the screen beside the TV. 'You caught him out of position again?'

'Yeah, a few times. I don't know why he won't just listen and do what we tell him.'

Al heaves himself up from the chair. 'I'd better go and see to him.'

From the bottom of the stairs he sees a light peeking under the door and turns back to the lounge. 'Jennifer! You left the main freakin light on!'

'I'm sorry, Al. It was just so dark in there.'

'It's *meant* to be dark, you idiot! We can see enough with just the lamp.'

'Al, Al, it's okay,' says Amanda. 'Best take the bulb out, then there'll be no mistakes.'

Al plops back down onto the sofa. 'I'll go up later. I'm too tired now.'

'Looks like he's falling asleep again,' says Amanda, pointing at the screen.

'He knows better than that,' roars Al. And he stamps up the stairs towards the starving boy in the attic.

Takoda age three – 2012 – seven years earlier

'Mommy, I'm hungry.'

She sighs.

'I'm sorry, Mommy.'

Grandma takes my hand. 'It's alright, Takoda. Mommy's sick today. I'll get you guys something to eat.'

'Is it that bad medicine she keeps taking?' says my older brother. 'Is that what makes her sick?'

Grandma nods.

'There's something else, Grandma,' I say.

'What's that, hon?'

'When Mommy isn't looking, that man hurts us.'

She turns to my mom. 'Robin, you got yourself another good for nothing boyfriend? Don't let anyone hurt the kids! You need to put a stop to this or you're gonna lose them.'

Mommy lies back in the chair. 'I know, I know. I really want to try and be a good mom.'

'When you're clean, you're a different person.'

'I do try, Mom. You know I do.' Mommy beckons me and my brother over to her. 'I need to try harder, I know that; for my beautiful boys.'

I snuggle into her arms. 'I love you, Mommy.'

'And I love you too, baby. I'm sorry I'm mean to you sometimes.'

I start to clamber onto her lap but she's too weak to help me up.

'I can't, Takoda,' she says.

Grandma sighs and lifts me into her arms instead. She ruffles my brother's hair. 'You're our beautiful boys, aren't you?'

Mommy is falling asleep again and Grandma turns on the TV. It's time for Sesame Street.

The next time the bad man beats on us, the welfare people tell us we can't be around Mommy and her boyfriend anymore. I'm glad we aren't going to be hurt now, but I'm sad too. If we don't see her so much, I'll miss Mommy. But when we get fostered out, we still spend time with Grandma and everyone, so I guess it's not so bad.

I just wish Mommy could come with us and be fostered too.

Takoda age five – 2014 – two years later

'Katie, I drew a picture for you.'

'Oh that's real nice, baby,' she says, and gives me a hug.

I grin and squeeze tight. 'Are you my real Mommy?'

'Oh, Takoda, you know better than that. You've got a real Mommy who still loves you, even though you don't live with her.'

'I know. She's a good Mommy, but she's sick.'

'And she might come back and take care of you, sweetheart.' She hands me a biscuit.

'That'd be good. But I like it here too,' I say.

'I know, baby.'

'If Mommy comes, that man won't come too, will he? He was a bad man and he hurt me.'

'You're right, Takoda. He was a bad man. No, he's gone away. He can't hurt you anymore. No one's gonna hurt you, baby.' She puts me down on the rug. 'Go play for a little while now.'

Katie turns to her fiancé. 'We need to get this sorted out, hon.'

'I'm trying. It's such a long process. I'll give them a call again tomorrow.'

Katie puts her arms around his waist. 'I can hardly wait till the adoption's final. Takoda can get settled and he'll be our son for real.'

'Hey, anybody home?'

'Grandma! It's Grandma,' I shout, dashing to the door.

'Whoa, there,' she laughs. 'You're about to knock me over. What a big boy you're getting!'

'Hi, Mrs S. How's it going?'

'Actually, I need to speak to you. Urgently.'

'Hey, Takoda. Go make Puppy his supper,' says Katie.

'Okay. But do I get to see Grandma later?'

'Course you do, baby. Just run along right now, okay?' She turns to Grandma. 'Sit down, Kelly. Now, what's going on?'

'It's Robin.'

'Well, I guessed that much,' says Katie. 'She in trouble again?'

'Big trouble. She got sent down this time.'

'Oh, shoot! Really?'

'That girl of mine. I don't know what we can do with her.'

'So what about the kids?'

'Can you still take care of that little man?'

'Sure, of course.'

'Listen, Katie. I heard his daddy means to come up and see the two boys.'

A shiver runs down Katie's back. 'No, that can't be right.'

The older woman shakes her head. 'It's what I heard, and I think it's gonna happen.'

'But he hasn't been interested in them at all! Why? Why now?'

'Men like McLean don't like to lose control of anything they think belongs to them. Look, let's wait and see, but I thought I'd better let you know.'

'I appreciate it. He won't take Takoda, will he?'

'Uh-uh. I don't think he can do that. Not after all this time.'

'Oh Lord, he's his Daddy though.'

I push my car across the rug and smile to myself. *My Daddy! My real Daddy's gonna come see me! He won't let any bad men beat on me.*

We're going to live with Daddy! He lives someplace far away, so we'll miss everyone, but we're kind of excited too. He's a big, strong man and he'll show us the things other Daddies teach their sons about how to grow up to be kind and clever.

Daddy lives with his girlfriend, Amanda, and they've got dogs we can play with and take for walks.

That's going to be pretty neat. I'm looking forward to going to a new school too.

'Hurry up. Get in. And what you crying for?'

'Sorry, Daddy. I wanted to say Goodbye to Grandma and everybody.'

'We don't have time for all that. Come on.'

The journey seems to take forever and I start to feel sick.

'Daddy, can we stop?'

Daddy turns to his girlfriend. 'We're hardly out of the state and the boy's getting on my nerves already. Can you shut him up?'

'I think I'm going to be sick, Daddy.'

My new house is pretty nice, even though it's not as clean and tidy as Grandma's house. I hear the dogs as soon as we open the door and I race my brother down to the basement to say 'Hi'. It smells real bad down there and I have to watch where I'm walking. The dogs are pretty friendly though.

Amanda makes us something to eat, then we all sit and watch TV.

Daddy is mad a lot of the time. A whole lot more than Mommy ever was. The cops have come to our door a bunch of times. Once he pulled Amanda along by her hair and said he was gonna kill her. He's not as nice to us as we thought he'd be, though we try our best to be good and not horse around. If he says we've been bad, he beats on us.

Horace Mann is a pretty good school, although I don't have any friends yet. The thing I like best is that they give me extra for breakfast and lunch so I don't always have to be hungry. When I first had to go to school in wet clothes, I got sent to the nurse and she washed me all up and gave me something dry to wear. When it was time for home, I made sure I got changed back into my own clothes so Daddy wouldn't know.

'Get the fuck out of bed, Takoda. Right now!' shouts Amanda.

Now that Daddy has started beating on me late at night, I can hardly wake up in the mornings. I'm not as good in school as I used to be either. 'Sorry, Amanda. I'm coming.'

'How come Caleb can get up and be ready but you have to take so long about it?'

'I don't know. I'm sorry.'

'You do these things just so I'll tell your Daddy so he can beat you.'

'No, honest I don't! Please don't tell Daddy.'

'You arguing with me, Takoda?'

'No, Ma'am. I'm sorry.'

That day, I fall over in the playground and hurt my knee. The nurse at the clinic is real gentle. It's the same one who washes my clothes sometimes. As I'm lying with my feet up on the couch she's got in there, I hear her on the phone.

'But Mr McLean, Takoda is hurt pretty bad. And when I examined him …'

I can hear Daddy yelling down the phone. 'Don't you touch my boys, do you hear me? Get him out of that clinic and back to class.'

'Well, okay, if he can manage to walk on it, I'll do that.'

'He *can* walk on it. Just tell him to get up and walk. Or put him on the damn phone to me, and I'll *make* him walk.'

'No, no it's fine. He's getting up off the bed right now. Can you manage okay, Takoda?'

'And stop being so damn soft with him. Just you make him do it, and that's it. You got that?'

She puts down the phone and turns to me. 'Those bruises I saw, Takoda. Did your dad do that to you?'

'I was being bad. I don't listen to him like I should.'

I go back to class and do my best to concentrate, but when I look out the window, I see Dad storming into the schoolyard. A few minutes later, the principal's assistant comes for me.

'Your dad is pretty mad,' she says, as she leads me towards the office. 'Just sit out here for a minute until you get called in.'

I reckon the whole school can hear my dad's voice. 'You need to STOP talking to my kids, right? You need to STOP giving them food, changing their clothes, treating them for things when there's nothing wrong with them. You need to STOP all that, right now!'

'Mr McLean, we take care of the children. It's part of our job, and when we see something isn't right, it's our legal duty to sort it out. Why do you want to let your kids suffer like this?'

'You said it right there, Lady. MY kids. I do what I want around MY kids. You got that? Damn boys're spending more time with that nurse than they do in class! And then nobody calls me to tell me what's going on.'

'I'm sorry you're angry, Sir, but we have to do these things. We can be sure to call you every time if that's what you want.'

'Sending them to the clinic, and calling Child Welfare on me! It ends now, do you hear me?'

I wish I could get away. I know Dad is going to beat me real bad. But I sit there, trying not to cry.

'And that time Caleb went running away? Was it y'all sent the cops to my door?'

'I don't know, Sir. I think when they found Caleb they needed to check how things were at home.'

'And then he shoots his mouth off, telling everybody I make him do squats and everything. You're damn right I do! Those kids need to learn how to behave themselves and mind their Daddy.'

It quietens down a little, and the principal and one of my teachers come out of the room. The door is still slightly open.

'You okay to go home with your dad, Takoda?'

I can see Dad glaring at me through the opening.

'Yes, I'm okay.'

The teacher pulls the door closed. 'You sure about that, Takoda?'

'Yes, I'm sure. I might get a spanking for bringing trouble though.'

'I can hear you, Takoda,' yells my dad. 'You keep that mouth shut.'

'Mr McLean, will you please be quiet for a moment.'

Dad comes out the door. 'Okay then, how about this? My son is sick. I'd better take him home,' and he grabs my hand and drags me down the corridor, away from school.

They come knocking a few days later, but Dad tells us not to make a sound, and after a while the knocking stops. I think they call again a few more times, but even the dogs know they'd better shut up.

After each visit, Dad is even more furious with me. 'You can't behave yourself in school, you can't GO to school,' he shouts.

'But Dad, I can't help it if they want to wash my clothes or put a band aid on my arm.'

'Get up those stairs and I'm coming to see to you in five minutes. You got that?'

I drag my feet. I hate it up there. The smelly old mattress turns my stomach, even though I stink just as bad myself. I hear Dad's footsteps and I wish there was somewhere to hide. But I'm surprised when he doesn't beat me this time.

For my punishment, all I have to do is stand up straight, then cross my legs, and bend forward to grip my ankles.

'Don't move till I come back up,' says Dad, locking the door behind him.

The relief at not getting beat soon wears off. After a few minutes, bending over like this is agony. My back, my arms and my legs are screaming out to relax. Bending my knees a little eases the burning in my calves, but the pain in my back doubles. After a while the whole thing is just unbearable. I straighten up and stretch out my back.

I'm so wrapped up in the feeling of relief that I don't hear Dad coming back up.

'What the fuck are you doing?' he yells. 'Didn't I tell you stay in that position until I told you to move?'

'I'm sorry, Dad. It was hurting real bad. I just couldn't hold it anymore.'

'That's a shame, son.' His voice is surprisingly gentle. 'I'll find a way to help with that.'

'I did try, Dad.'

'I know. Just get some sleep now, and we'll finish off tomorrow.'

'Here? You want me to sleep in here?'

'Sure. There's a mattress right there for you. Do not leave this room. You got that?'

'But what if I need the bathroom?'

'Don't leave this room. Night night.'

As the door closes I look around and realise how dark the room is. There's a small window but it hardly lets in any light, especially at this time of night. Apart from the mattress, a dirty lawn chair, and an old wooden stool, the room is empty. I just know I'm going to need to go to the bathroom. Thinking about it makes it worse, and after about an hour, I'm desperate to go. I check the door, and Dad's forgotten to lock it, but I daren't creep downstairs after what Dad told me. And nobody hears my banging on the floor to be allowed to get out, so I have to do it in my shorts.

The next day, it doesn't sound like Dad's gone out to work, cos I can hear him hammering and banging, as if he's doing some DIY. Maybe he's fixing the cupboard in the kitchen. He comes up the stairs, carrying his toolbox, and I ask him if I can go down and use the bathroom, and he tells me that's okay, and to wash my shorts in the bathtub while I'm down there. I rub them as well as I can, and wonder what I'm supposed to wear now.

'Get back up here, Takoda,' shouts Dad, just as I'm wringing them out.

I go up as quick as I can, cos Dad doesn't like to be kept waiting.

He gathers his tools together and packs them back in the box. 'I still didn't punish you properly for making those inspectors come snooping around.' He throws me on the bed and I catch sight of the metal spatula Amanda sometimes uses in the kitchen. It hurts so much.

'Dad,' I scream. 'Dad, please stop.'

'Shut up,' he says.

I can't stop screaming though.

'I thought I told you to shut the fuck up! You don't listen to me, I'm going to make you listen.' And he makes me do the punishment position again, with the blood dripping down my legs making it hard to grip them.

'You gonna behave yourself today, Takoda? You gonna stay like that till I tell you it's enough?' He turns the door handle. 'Because if you don't, I'll know about it.'

What does he mean? How will he know if I move? I guess I manage a little longer than yesterday, but pretty soon I have to relieve the pressure on my limbs and my back.

Dad runs up the stairs quicker than I've ever known. 'Back into position,' he roars, before going downstairs again. This happens on and off all day long. My muscles are screaming in pain, but I keep having to get into position time after time. I can smell cooking, and hear the faint sound of the TV. When I move slightly to try and ease the pain, Dad bounds upstairs again.

'Stand up,' he orders, and I arch backwards in a blissful stretch.

'Thanks, Dad.'

He grabs my arm and drags me down the stairs and into the living room. I'm hardly ever allowed in there these days. The TV is blaring away, but he points to another screen right beside it. 'We know every move you make, Takoda. So when you don't listen to me and do what I tell you, I can see it all!'

I peer at the split screen. One shows the bed and the other shows the place on the floor where I have to do 'the position'.

'Maybe that'll make you think twice when you decide to move after I've told you to keep still.'

I look from my dad towards Amanda and back again.

'We'll be watching you 24/7,' says Dad. 'Oh, and I forgot to mention, you won't be going back to school. You're being homeschooled now.'

Daddy and Amanda laugh.

Homeschool. No teachers looking out for me and giving me food. No nurses bathing my wounds or giving me clean clothes to wear. And I bet Dad is a strict teacher when we get started.

Turns out, Dad isn't a strict teacher. He isn't a teacher at all. No books, no pencils, no chalkboard. Nothing. My days are filled with nothing. When I'm excused from the punishment poses, I bang my head against the wall in frustration. They call me a dirty dog when I soil my shorts or the mattress, but they don't allow me to use the bathroom all day.

'You think you can manage them? I mean Takoda is real bad. He won't listen and behave himself,' says Amanda.

Her sister, Jennifer, shuffles in her seat. 'Well, I think I can manage a couple of kids.'

'You have to make sure they do what Al tells them. And let him know when they don't. You okay with that?'

'Sure. That's no problem. Just as long as I can bring my dog, I'm good.'

'What do you think, Al?' says Amanda. 'I think she'll be okay. She does what I tell her anyways.'

Daddy narrows his eyes at Jennifer. 'Don't you disappoint me now, or you'll be out on the street.'

'Takoda, get here and say 'Hi' to Jennifer,' says Amanda.

I'm excited to have another grown-up in the house. Maybe she'll stop Daddy from hurting us so bad, but then I see that same empty look in her eyes as Amanda. 'Hi, Jennifer.'

Dad tells her what a bad boy I am and that I don't listen to him and do the things I'm supposed to do. 'He's crazy, Jennifer. Even eats his own shit.'

He doesn't tell her that it's Daddy who makes me do it. After a few times, I started to do it myself so he doesn't beat me so much for making a mess.

'Gross,' she says, looking at me in disgust.

When Dad takes us both upstairs and shows her how I have stay to bent over, she says, 'Oh yes, I've seen that on TV; it's called a *stress position*, they use it to torture people.'

Dad laughs. 'I like that! I wonder what else they do!'

'How long does he stay like that?' says Jennifer.

'Just a few hours.'

'Wow! That's pretty good.'

Jennifer stays home all day and keeps house while Dad and Amanda are out at work. She minds Al's little brother, and I hear her speaking to him softly. That makes me cry, because I remember Mommy talking to me like that sometimes when she wasn't sick. Nobody talks to me like that anymore.

Jennifer reads books and watches TV, but a lot of the time, she's watching me. When I move, she yells up the stairs, 'Takoda! I'll have to tell your dad!' She doesn't really talk to me except to tell me the trouble I'm going to get into. Sometimes she looks at me and asks why I put on such a show, and I don't know what she means. 'Why don't you listen to your dad?'

But Dad punishes me for reasons I don't understand, and no matter how much I listen and try to behave myself, he beats me anyway.

Time passes real slow up here. I wait and wait for it to get dark and someone to tell me I can lie down, so I can try to sleep. But if he's had a bad day at work, Dad gets me up again, and I have to leave my dream to get beat and go back into 'the position'.

The window is small. I'm skinny and kind of weak, but I climb up onto the stool and push against the glass. It opens. The voices I can usually hear in the street below get louder and I can see cars going by. It's a long time since I've seen a car. It's now or never. I scramble up over the frame and grip onto the sides to steady myself. It seems a long way down.

'Takoda. Takoda, you can wake up now.'

I slowly open my eyes, and a strange lady dressed in white is looking down on me. *Am I in Heaven?* I must have said that out loud because the lady is smiling and shaking her head.

'No, sweetheart. You're in the hospital.'

I feel a pillow under my head and look down at the clean sheets. 'Am I sick?'

The lady smiles and points to a plaster cast suspended in the air. 'Don't you remember, Takoda? You fell from the window and you've broken your leg. You're staying here until it gets better. Do you think you're about ready to try something to eat? We've got broth or burgers. We've even got fries today.'

I start to cry. I'm staying here! I'm staying in this comfortable bed and getting fries to eat. I cry so hard the lady puts her arms around me and kisses the top of my head.

'Shh, honey. You're safe. We're gonna take real good care of you.'

'Get your hands off my son!' Dad strides down the ward, and for a minute I think he's going to slap the nurse.

She drops her arms but takes my hand. 'He was crying, Mr McLean.'

'Hah, crying! I'll give him something to cry about.' He nudges my sore leg and I yell out.

'Mr McLean! You'd better stop that!'

In a flash, two security guards appear and lead my dad out of the ward.

He's back the next day to take me home.

The window is boarded up, and Dad has built a partition so the room is half the size it was. There's a new lock on the door.

I don't know where my big brother has gone. With all the pain I was going through, I almost forgot he might be somewhere in the house, suffering too. But I realise I haven't seen or heard him for a long time.

Most days, Jennifer gets me up around 7am and I go downstairs, where she lets me use the bathroom, and I wash my shorts in the tub where I have messed them the day before. She doesn't speak to me, except when I stumble around, when she tells me to quit putting on a show. I get something to eat and drink and go back and eat it in my room. There's never enough, and I'm starving most of the time.

After that, I hear the rest of the family getting up and Al's little brother giggling as he splashes in the bathtub.

I get into my position and have to stay like that until the next day, at around 3am. Dad has got hold of a taser now and the pain is the worst. My muscles cramp up and I fall to the ground. It makes me go to the bathroom in my shorts, but that's nothing unusual now. He does something horrible to my butt too, and I bleed and shit everywhere and I get blamed for making a mess and not listening to what he tells me.

I don't think there's any way to escape.

I've been allowed to come into the lounge. When I hear her voice on the phone, I remember her straight away. 'Mommy,' I whisper. 'Are you coming for me?'

'Oh, baby. I'd sure like to. Is your daddy looking after you good?'

No one is near, so I tell Mommy about being locked in my room.

'They just let you out to go to school?'

'I don't go to school anymore, Mommy. Daddy and Amanda are supposed to teach me.'

I hear Mommy gasp.

'Mommy, he whips me with his belt. I jumped out of the window, and …'

'That's enough now, Takoda,' yells Daddy from the family room.

'I have to go now, Mommy.'

'I love you, baby. Let me talk to Daddy.'

But Dad just comes over and slams the phone down.

Dad has punched me in the stomach about 100 times today, and I feel so bad. I've thrown up once or twice, and it's mostly my own shit that comes out of my mouth. Finally, he lets me go to sleep.

When Jennifer calls me down the next morning I can hardly move, but somehow I manage to stagger down the stairs, though I'm screaming with the pain.

'Shut up! You'll wake your dad! Come on, hurry up.'

Dad comes out of his bedroom. 'You filthy piece of shit, stop making that noise! Get back upstairs!'

And I have to get myself up there again. Dad follows me. I can't hold myself up, so Dad drags me around the room, and then, as I'm laid flat on my stomach, I feel him stand on my back.

'Dad, I can't breathe,' I whisper.

But his weight presses down on me harder and harder. Then he throws me on the bed and I scream and scream as he pushes something right up my butt and presses it deep inside.

'Help me, help me,' I'm crying, until I'm so weak with the pain, I can't yell anymore. Dad throws the thing into the corner and I see the leg of the stool, bloody and covered in my shit. I feel like I'm going to pass out and I'm only half aware that Dad is dragging me downstairs again.

'Now get those filthy shorts washed real good,' he shouts. 'Or, I swear I'll drown you, you dirty dog.'

I have no strength left. Dad shoves my head under the water, and I splash and try to get my head up. When he yanks me up I gasp for air before he puts me under again. And again. And again.

An Overview of Takoda's Case

Takoda Collins
18.12.08 – 13.12.19
aged 10 years & 11 months
Ohio, USA

Takoda was born in Wisconsin, to Robin Collins and Al-Mutahan McLean. (In some reports on the case, McLean is shown with the alternative spelling of Mclean.)

Although Robin Collins had custody of her son, and she saw him often, her drug addiction meant that she was not able to care for him full time, and the baby was entrusted to the care of a friend and her fiancé.

When Takoda was 11 months old, his mother's boyfriend spanked him so severely that Children's Services launched an investigation, which resulted in Robin Collins losing custody of Takoda, and the little boy was placed in foster care for the next three years. In 2011, when her son was aged three, Collins was sent to prison for drug offences.

Around this time, McLean posted on his Facebook page: *Wish I could spend time with my boys.* It is unclear whether he actually saw Takoda at all until he was four years old, at which time McLean visited Wisconsin, took a DNA test which proved he was his father, and eventually took the boy into his full custody in October 2013.

McLean already had a history of violence. Records show that he once punched a man he believed had stolen his phone, and he was accused of hitting his fiancée, Amanda Hinze, over the head with a pipe, dragging her by her hair and punching her. The charges were later dismissed.

Robin Collins appealed to the court several times to prevent McLean from taking her son out of state. However, in June 2014, she signed a notarised letter, agreeing to allow a move to Pennsylvania. A few days later, she wrote a handwritten letter saying that she had been bullied and coerced into doing so.

But McLean and Takoda had already gone.

After a number of house moves, McLean and his son(s) took up residence at the home of his girlfriend, Amanda Hinze, on Kensington Drive, Dayton, Ohio. During 2016 and beyond, the police were called to the property several times, following reports of violence against Hinze, and for sundry neighbour disputes. But nothing came of them.

On 20 August 2016, Takoda's older brother ran away, but was later found, and he told police about the various punishments his father made him endure, including being forced to do squats while holding a heavy backpack. Police contacted Children's Services and were told that a referral had been made. But their attempt to search the property was hampered by the aggression of the pit bull dogs, and all areas could not be accessed.

During the visit, when questioned about a number of cameras in place around the home, McLean claimed that they were just for show.

Concerned staff at Horace Mann, the school Takoda attended for around two years, tried to show the boy kindness and care. They ensured he was given extra food to eat, and when he arrived in urine-soaked shorts, they gave him clean clothes to wear. They later remarked that the little boy seemed starved of attention and affection, that he was emotional, and often sad and crying, saying that Takoda would "separate himself from other students and just stand and cry".

McLean balked their endeavours at every turn, and he certainly did not want staff questioning his son. He would ring or visit the school in fury that Takoda had been taken into the clinic to be changed after having a bathroom accident. As part of the 'Friday Backpack Program', Takoda was given food to take home. McLean made another phone call: "My son will not bring food home from school!"

We have seen this many times–an abusive parent demanding that others who could relieve their child's suffering refrain from helping them.

Staff were caught between a rock and a hard place. Takoda became increasingly terrified of staff calling his father, but McLean insisted that they call him about every incident. It seems he wanted to know exactly what was going on, perhaps in order to have further flimsy grounds on which to punish the little boy. Several calls were made to Montgomery County Children's Services, and one staff member recalls phoning 911 after McLean called his son out from school, claiming that the boy was sick.

In common with many abused children who are powerless at home, Takoda occasionally exhibited slightly aggressive behaviour at school, such as stepping in front of another kid in line, or stopping them from having a turn on the swings, but when teachers said they'd have to call his dad, he'd beg them not to.

On 11 May 2018, Dayton Public Schools & Montgomery County Child Services requested a police visit to the home, fearing for Takoda's welfare. Within days, he was pulled from school, and school staff say they never saw the boy again.

On 31 July 2018, Takoda was formally withdrawn, to be homeschooled.

Although both Children's Services and the police were alerted to the suspected abuse, reports are sketchy as to the outcome of visits made, and they sometimes left when no one answered the door.

For four years, Robin Collins did not know where her son was. Only when McLean was caught drunk driving in Dayton, Ohio, did she discover their location, and she finally got to speak to Takoda on the phone in May 2019. What she heard frightened her, and the following day, Collins filed a motion for contempt against McLean, reporting that he had broken the terms of their custody agreement, having never brought Takoda to see her, and that in four years, she had spoken to her son only once on the phone, the previous day.

As Robin Collins resided in Wisconsin, to whom she made the complaint, and Takoda lived in Ohio, the motion was dismissed, on the grounds that Takoda did not reside in the state of Wisconsin, and it was therefore not their responsibility.

The next day, a desperately worried Collins made a 911 call, reporting that Takoda's father was abusing him and begging them to talk to her son without his father present.

She told them that the custody agreement had not been adhered to, and related what was happening to her son:

"I've spoken with him (Takoda) one time in the last four years and that was two days ago.

"Our custody agreement is that he's (McLean) supposed to bring him back to the state four times a year. I'm supposed to have phone conversations with him (Takoda) once a week, talk to his school and talk to his doctors. He has not abided by the court order.

"He's locked him in his room and he tried to jump out a window. He sent him to school in a diaper. He's pulled him out of school. He whips them with a belt. Just a bunch of stuff that's very concerning to me.

"It's just very demeaning and very vulgar*. I don't really know if he's telling the truth or not, but even if he's not, I would feel much better knowing that a police officer pulled my son to the side and talked to him one-on-one to make sure that nothing is going on. He (McLean) won't let me talk to him and when he does let me talk to him he stands over him on the phone and tells him what to say."

* This leads me to believe that Takoda had disclosed to his mother at least part of the abuse relating to his private areas, including the abuse with objects, enforced soiling of his clothes, and being made to consume faeces.

This phone call to the police could have made the difference between life and death for Takoda Collins, but despatch records say that they believed he was being cared for. Records don't say whether Children's Services were contacted.

Robin Collins often gets bad press. And it is sadly true that if she hadn't been using, McLean would not have got custody of Takoda and his sibling(s). However, she was an addict, and tragically, having children didn't result in her being able to turn her life around until it was too late for Takoda.

But if either Children's Services or the police had acted upon the information Collins gave them, there is every chance that Takoda would have lived.

McLean's girlfriend, Amanda Hinze, owned the property they all lived in, and was the chief breadwinner, often working six days a week at Walgreens, on the 2–11pm shift. Acting as Takoda's stepmother, she should have taken care of the little boy's physical, psychological, emotional, and educational needs. Clearly she failed.

Questioned under caution, she remained largely non-committal, but, obviously concerned that Ebert might reveal too much, Hinze was quick to claim that her sister had a learning disability.

Pointing to the photos of Takoda's wounds, the detective asserted that she must have known that he was miserable all that time, especially as she allegedly homeschooled him.

"What monster does this? Are you a monster?"

"No."

"Okay, then tell me how this happened?"

"I don't know. He was usually wearing clothes when I saw him."

"What about his arms, his hands, his face, his head?"

Hinze had no answer.

Detective Schloss asked where his clothes were kept, and Hinze was forced to admit that most of them had been thrown out. Schloss eventually lost patience with Hinze, presumably due in part to her lack of emotion that the little boy has just died. Schloss told her there was no place for "stupid" right now.

On the day of the murder, Hinze said that she left the house at 1pm to run errands, along with her sister. Despite the bank she planned to visit being open until 6pm, she was in such a hurry that she was still in her pyjamas, and admitted that she hadn't even taken the time to clean her teeth.

Hinze set up a GoFundMe account on Facebook to raise money for a memorial, saying that Takoda: *Passed away five days before his 11th birthday*. The page was later taken down.

Hinze's sister, Jennifer Ebert, also warrants our scrutiny.

When her mother would not allow her daughter's beloved blue-nose pit bull terrier to live in her home, Ebert found refuge for herself and her pet with her sister. Ebert's role was to take care of the Dayton home (and a child, McLean's three-year-old brother), whilst Hinze and McLean were out at work, and to report Takoda's misbehaviour to his father.

Jennifer Ebert's arrival brought no comfort or respite to Takoda. She adhered to instructions to make sure Takoda was still awake when Hinze returned home at 11pm and if he wasn't, McLean would "go berserk" at the little boy. Ebert further isolated Takoda by refusing to speak to him when she felt that he wasn't listening to her, yet she cared for the three-year-old in a relatively normal manner.

Dismissing Takoda's agony as disrespect for his father's orders, she repeatedly enforced McLean's instructions that his son spend 20 hours of every day, *for one or two years*, in torture positions. When questioned by the police, Ebert demonstrated the poses, standing, with crossed legs, hands behind the back, or bent forward, hands touching the floor, or crouched with arms out to the side. When asked why he had to do this, she said it was so that he would start listening and not do things he wasn't supposed to do, like going to the bathroom on himself. (There was no bathroom in the upstairs room in which Takoda was imprisoned.)

Ebert repeatedly told the police that she believed Takoda was deliberately "dancing around" and not walking straight, in order to make his father mad and punish him. After Takoda's break for freedom, and the partitioning of the attic room, Ebert witnessed the punishments being ramped up. In addition to having no access to the window, and being made to sleep under a tarp in the now half-size room, Takoda was more savagely beaten, thrown around the room, made to eat faeces, half-strangled, tasered for up to 20 seconds at a time, and subjected to having hot sauce poured onto his genitals.

When asked if she'd heard Takoda screaming on the day of his death, Ebert states: "I just figured it was another one of those days that he just didn't listen – he always just falls over even when he's laying in bed he just falls out of it and so he just likes putting on shows. He just likes getting into trouble."

Takoda gave up his fight for life on 13 December 2019.

At around 6:45am that morning, Ebert called Takoda downstairs as usual. And as usual, when he stumbled, and held onto the walls for balance, she decided he was playing up to get attention. When he reached the bathroom, he fell forward over the bathtub.

Ebert warned him to stop playing like he was sick, otherwise he would wake up his dad. McLean duly appeared from his bedroom at around 7:30am, and ordered his son back upstairs for punishment for his stumbling around. On the monitor, Ebert witnessed McLean standing on Takoda with all his weight, holding the ceiling so he could press down even harder. She watched Takoda being tossed and dragged around on the floor, then being put on the bed to have hot sauce poured over his buttocks.

In her police interview, Ebert claimed she didn't see much else, but she looks extremely uncomfortable when questioned about McLean sodomising his son with the leg of the stool.

McLean then dragged Takoda down the stairs and told his son that if he didn't wash his shorts properly he was going to drown him. Ebert heard splashing and Takoda gasping for air.

While Takoda was fighting for his life, Ebert continued to care for the three-year-old, before going to bed for a nap. A while later, she was woken by her sister, who told her that Takoda wasn't breathing.

Turning their backs on Takoda once again, the sisters grabbed the toddler and quickly left the house. They made no attempt to call for help.

Finally, McLean called 911, complaining about what a terrible child Takoda was, and how difficult he was to parent.

When the emergency crews arrived, Takoda was unresponsive, and was later pronounced dead at Dayton Children's Hospital. Informed that his child had died, McLean's response was: "Alright, I tried to get you guys here as fast as I could". Al-Mutahan McLean was arrested.

When questioned, McLean blamed Takoda for his own abuse, saying he shoved the chair leg up his own rectum and ate his own faeces. He had previously claimed that his son had psychiatric problems (of which, no doubt, McLean was the cause), and appeared to seek help for him. However, when it transpired that the help would consist of therapy rather than punishment, McLean refused to pursue this avenue. There was to be no comfort or help for Takoda.

Following McLean's arrest, Ebert and Hinze returned to the house and cleared out the attic, removing as much incriminating evidence as they could, including metal spatulas, tasers, a blood-stained mattress, etc.

And on 16 December 2019, police acquired a warrant to search the home, locating several items they believe were used in child abuse, including a taser, four taser-style dog collars, and a combination lock located in the attic. A broken-off chair leg was found in the laundry basket.

Hinze and Ebert were subsequently arrested for their part in Takoda's abuse.

All cases of children abused to death are horrific. And the torture of Takoda Collins goes beyond the bounds of humanity; sleep deprivation, stress positions, savage beatings, and defilement with an object. The prosecution attested that Takoda had suffered years of abuse at the hands of his father, with a pre-sentencing memo being entitled: '*Takoda Collins' Nightmare Existence*'. And that's exactly what it was.

The defendants claimed that Takoda's wounds were self inflicted. But the coroner's report told a different story. It revealed that whilst Takoda's visible wounds were shocking enough, with hundreds of abrasions and contusions of old and new injuries to the head and torso, there were also deep bruises, multiple rib fractures, and bruising inside the entire thickness of the gluteus maximus with swelling right down to the bone. "On his back there was a type of branding of four letters that appeared to begin with the letter T. This is, by its location, an area that would be unreachable, and is thus wholly inconsistent with self-infliction." I cannot find any further definitive information on this branding.

Takoda's entire digestive system was found to contain a tan yellow puree-like substance, both in his stomach and his bowels. This confirmed that when he had no choice but to defecate in the locked room, Takoda had initially been forced by his father to consume his own faeces, but as time went on, knowing he would have to do so anyway, it seems that he began to consume his bodily waste of his own volition.

The Montgomery County Coroner's office said that Takoda died as a result of blunt force trauma, in combination with compressive asphyxia and water submersion.

- McLean, aged 32, pleaded guilty to murder, rape and kidnapping, and three counts of child endangerment. He was sentenced to 51 years to life.
- Hinze, 30, and Ebert, 27, pleaded guilty to involuntary manslaughter and child endangerment. Hinze was handed down 22 years, and Ebert 8 years.

At the time of his death, Children's Services said they didn't have an open case on Takoda.

Rest Safely in Peace, Takoda

Are They Monsters?

The torture McLean inflicted upon his son can only be described as monstrous. And when I welcome new members to my Readers' List, I love to find out whether you think the perpetrators of these hideous acts are monsters, and if so, were they born this way?

It's the age-old *nature versus nurture* question, and some of you have pretty strong views.

I wonder what *you* think?

Perhaps you have gleaned from reading my books that I think very few perpetrators are born evil. It seems possible that they may have a propensity for it, but I feel that their life experiences influence which direction they take. Each horrific case I research makes me wonder what causes such inhumane behaviour, and McLean is one of the worst examples I have ever found.

But as always, with a view to preventing children's suffering, I want to know if McLean's upbringing made him the way he became. Unfortunately, I can find little information about McLean's childhood. (I have found an unsubstantiated report that when, as a child, he was always putting his fingers into his mouth, McLean's father used hot sauce on them as a method of prevention–which is echoed in McLean pouring hot sauce onto Takoda's anus.)

It seems that McLean was capable of love, as by all accounts, his young brother, who lived with him, was cherished, and there were family photographs all around the Dayton residence (though none of Takoda). Apparently, McLean had gained custody of his much younger brother when their mother (about whom it would be interesting to have more information) left the baby with her sister, who in due course passed the infant onto McLean.

Whatever one's view on the existence of 'monsters', I can't help but wonder how it is humanly possible to ram a chair leg up a little boy's rectum, and abuse him mercilessly every single day? Sadly, as I research more and more cases, I find that this form of torture is not unique to McLean–you will discover similarly evil acts in the free book I offer you.

Was the real monster Amanda Hinze? Without her cooperation, would McLean have escalated the abuse of his son to such horrific proportions? And had Hinze not taken the 'mother' role upon herself, giving the semblance of a normal family, preparing the documents that allowed Takoda to be 'homeschooled', etc, is it possible that he would have lived?

And what of Jennifer Ebert? When she was arrested a few days after Takoda's death, she was wearing a T-shirt emblazoned with the words: "*I'd help, but I don't want to*". Was she showing her true colours?

But is Ebert 'merely' guilty of indifference to the suffering of others? Of colossal selfishness in valuing her desire to keep her dog over speaking up on behalf of an abused child? Of stupidity, in believing that Takoda wanted to be tortured? Of being so gullible that she believed everything Al and Amanda told her?

Whatever the truth of the matter, she is certainly guilty of standing by and allowing (and watching) a child's agony to continue unabated, until he finally gave up the fight.

It feels appropriate to end this volume with Takoda's story. His case encompasses some of the most horrendous physical and psychological abuse I ever hope to uncover.

This torture did not take place in a concentration camp during a bloody war. Nor in a serial killer's lair.

But in a seemingly ordinary American home.

I am honoured that several of my readers have reached out to tell me that they endured abuse as children. They have broken the cycle to become loving parents. Doing so is a tremendous achievement, and a reason for hope.

Please don't feel guilty if you 'enjoy' my books. Most people tell me they feel a mixture of emotions, and I'm grateful you are reading, and are not one of the many who are unable to face the reality of the suffering taking place right under our noses.

> If you've been moved by the children's stories and would like to help me raise awareness, a **star rating or review** for this book enables new readers to find my books.

And I'd love to hear from you–if you have any comments or suggestions, please get in touch on:

jessicajackson@jesstruecrime.com

Help To Protect Children ...

like Elisa, Ame, Dennis, Poppie, Gabrielly and Takoda.

Please review in your usual way, or the QR code or link will help you to get back to the book's page:

https://mybook.to/Abused-To-Death-3

Then scroll waaay down
until you see Write a Review
(usually on the left side)

> Reviews help to spread awareness of abuse.
> Just a star rating or a few words is enough.

If you prefer, there are direct 'Easy Review Codes' at the back of this book, which take you where you need to be.

This book is dedicated to the memory of:
Elisa, Ame, Dennis, Poppie, Gabrielly and Takoda.

Your Next Book in the Series

Are you ready for more stories like these?

Abused To Death Volume 4

including the stories of these children:

- Adrian endured unspeakable torture, and after his death, his body was fed to pigs
- Hana was adopted from Ethiopia by those who believed they were doing God's work
- Max was hidden away year after year in a filthy attic

Please be aware – this book includes some of my most controversial writing.

Scan this code:

Or use this link:
https://mybook.to/Abused-To-Death-4

Join Us On Facebook

After I'd built up a following, with discussions and photos, to honour the murdered children ...

Facebook suspended my Page without explanation.

And everything is gone.

So please **Follow Me** and help me to start again!

Just scan this code:

Or use this link:

<u>Jessica Jackson Writer</u>

Or within Facebook, type into the search bar:

Jessica Jackson Writer

Can We Prevent These Murders?

There are no easy solutions, but these are my own views, which I cover in the pages of my books, echoing the advice of the World Health Organisation (WHO).

1 - End physical discipline of children
2 - Regulate homeschooling effectively
3 - An outlet for caregivers' anger
4 - Listen to the children when they report abuse
5 - Improve communication between agencies
6 - Safe places for unwanted babies
7 - Educate the parents of the future:
- that a baby communicates by crying
- how to give love, safety and guidance
- about bladder & bowel habits of children

In an ideal world, children would not be brought into an environment where drugs and/or violence abound, or where they are unwanted, or are wanted only to meet the impossible-to-meet needs of a parent. But to protect the ones who are already born, we need adequate support, education and a joined-up system where an abused child does not fall through the cracks.

Warning Signs of Abuse

There are various factors that might suggest a child is being abused. This list has been compiled by the NSPCC, but is by no means exhaustive:

- unexplained changes in behaviour or personality
- becoming withdrawn or anxious
- becoming uncharacteristically aggressive
- lacking social skills and having few friends
- poor bonding or relationship with a parent
- knowledge of adult issues inappropriate for their age
- running away or going missing
- wearing clothes which cover their body

And I would add:

- marks and bruises on the body
- being secretive
- stealing (often food)
- weight loss
- inappropriate clothing
- poor hygiene / unkempt appearance
- tiredness
- inability to concentrate
- being overly eager to please the adult
- the child telling you that they're being hurt
- a non-verbal child showing you that they're being hurt

- the adult removing the child from school after they have come under suspicion

If you suspect an adult of abusing a child, don't unquestioningly accept what they say, but instead:

        A - Assume nothing

        B - Be vigilant

        C - Check everything

        D - Do something

Listen to the children and report what you see:

To report child abuse in the USA & Canada

The National Child Abuse Hotline:1-800-422-4453
If a child is in immediate danger, call 911

To report child abuse in the UK

For adults, call the NSPCC on 0808 800 5000
For children, call Childline on 0800 1111
Or if there is risk of imminent danger, ring 999

To report child abuse in Australia

The National Child Abuse Reportline: 131-478
Children, call: 1800-55-1800
If a child is in immediate danger, call 000

Find All My Books on Amazon

Find them in your usual way, or you can …

Search Amazon for:

Abused To Death by Jessica Jackson

Or scan this code:

Or use this link:

https://viewbook.at/abused-series

I'd love you to **Follow** me on Amazon too!

Don't Miss A Thing

Pick up your free ebook:

Just scan this code:

https://BookHip.com/KXACJDT

Follow me on Facebook:

Jessica Jackson Writer

Follow me on Amazon:

https://author.to/jessicajackson

*(Ensure your Settings in **Communications / Preferences in Amazon** are set to receive info about new releases.)*

Easy Review Codes

It's quick & easy - just a star rating or a few words is all it takes

For Amazon.com
(US, NZ, SA, etc)

For Amazon in the UK

For Amazon in Canada

For Amazon in Australia

Or find it in your usual way

Thank you very much x

Acknowledgments

WITH GRATEFUL THANKS TO:

- My beta readers: Jackson, Linda and Rick
- All my email subscribers, old and new
- My Facebook followers
- My incredible Advance Readers
- My fellow authors who generously promote my books:

  True crime writers, Ryan Green, Jason Neal, and Ben Oakley

  Memoir writers, Lynn Walker and Toni Maguire

  And for much needed light relief, my friend and comedy crime writer, Roy M Burgess

JESSICA JACKSON

Selected Resources
For Elisa, Ame, Dennis, Poppie, Takoda & Gabrielly

Cinderella and The Prince
Elisa Izquierdo,
New York, USA
aged 6
Died 1995

Abandoned To Her Fate
David Van Biema - Time Magazine - 24.06.01
Little Lost Girl
Rolonda Watts interview with Awilda Lopez - April 1996
The Death Of Little Elisa
Marc Peyser - Newsweek 12.10.95

The Family
Ame Deal
Arizona, USA
aged 10
Died 2011

Forget Me Not: Ame Lynn Deal
Suffer The Little Children Blog - 19.04.20
Ame Deal Murder Trial
12 News via Youtube - July 2017
Podcast 64 - Ame Deal
Morbidology - Emily Thompson - 07.10.20

The Perfect Mother
Dennis Jurgens
Minnesota, USA
aged 3
Died 1965

Jury told adoptive mother abused boy before his death
Suzanne Malich - apnews.com - 13.05.87
Child Murder - The town that lived in silence
Barry Siegel - latimes.com - 28.02.88
State v Jurgens
Court of Appeals Minnesota - law.justia.com - 06.07.88

Playing Dead
Poppie Van der Merwe
Brits, South Africa
aged 3
Died 2016

Suffer The Little Children Podcast Episode 50 & 51
Laine - 17.02.21
Poppie is playing dead again
Jana van der Merwe - news24.com (YOU) - 09.11.17
South African Cities Week
Dennis Webster in Orania - theguardian.com - 24.10.19

Surveillance
Takoda Collins,
Ohio, USA
aged 10
Died 2019

Unimaginable, Constant Torture on Murdered Child
Jerry Lambe - Law & Crime - 28.09.21 (inc Prosecutor's Memo)
A Friend To Everyone - The Death of Takoda Hayden Collins
Phoenixx Fyre Dean - Vocal Media - June 2022
Jennifer Ebert Confession
Demand News, YouTube - 09.01.23

If You Tell - Buried Alive
Gabrielly
Magalhães Souza,
Brasilândia, Brazil
aged 10
Died 2020

In Loving Memory of Little Gabrielly Magalhães de Souza
Facebook Group
Buried Alive - The True, Terrifying Story of Gabrielly Magalhães
The Odditorium, YouTube - 17.10.22
Emileide, accused of killing her daughter is scheduled for January
André Frederico - cicadaoms.com/br —08.12.21

Disclaimer

My aim is to tell stories of murdered children with a combination of accuracy and readability, to heighten awareness of child torture and murder, and to explore ways of preventing further tragedies. I have relied on the factual information available to me during my research, and where I have added characters or dramatised events to better tell the child's story, I believe I have done so without significantly altering the important details. If anyone has further information about the children, particularly if you knew them and have anecdotes to share about their life, I would be delighted to hear from you. Likewise, whilst every attempt has been made to make contact with copyright holders, if I have unwittingly used any material when I was not at liberty to do so, please contact me so that this can be rectified at:

jessicajackson@jesstruecrime.com

Printed in Dunstable, United Kingdom